"A stimulatingly counter-intuitive take on the state of British Christianity, it should be read by anyone – believer or non-believer – who is interested in the future of religion in Britain."

> – **TOM HOLLAND, author of *Millennium*, *In the Shadow of the Sword*, and *Dynasty***

"This book offers a timely word of encouragement to British Christians and a robust challenge to the narrative of church decline that has seized the minds of many British commentators on religion and sapped the spiritual energies of many British Christians. It reveals weaknesses in the decline narrative, exposes the reasons why evidence of church growth is neglected, and draws attention to the many ways in which churches contribute effectively to the common good of British society. Readers may not agree with every critique or proposal in the book, but anyone who has been enticed by the story of the decline of British Christianity will be forced to review their evidence and their assumptions."

> – **DR JONATHAN CHAPLIN, Director of the Kirby Laing Institute for Christian Ethics, Tyndale House, Cambridge**

"This small book raises big questions that need to be addressed. You will find in these pages provocative and challenging analysis. Have a read and then join the debate!"

> – **DR KRISH KANDIAH, President of the London School of Theology**

T0311180

GOD'S
UNWELCOME
RECOVERY

WHY THE NEW ESTABLISHMENT WANTS TO PROCLAIM THE DEATH OF FAITH

SEAN OLIVER-DEE

MONARCH
BOOKS

Oxford UK, and Grand Rapids, USA

Published by Monarch Books
an imprint of
Lion Hudson plc
Wilkinson House, Jordan Hill Road,
Oxford OX2 8DR, England
Email: monarch@lionhudson.com
www.lionhudson.com/monarch

ISBN 978 0 85721 630 4
e-ISBN 978 0 85721 631 1

First edition 2015

Acknowledgments
Biblical quotations are from the Holy Bible: New International Version, anglicised edition, copyright © 1973, 1978, 1984, 2011 by Biblica Inc. Used by permission of Hodder & Stoughton, a member of the Hodder Headline Group. All rights reserved.
pp. 39–40: Extract from "London: a rising island of religion in a secular sea?" by Eric Kaufman copyright © 2006, Eric Kaufman. Reprinted by permission of Demos.
pp. 82–83, 110: Extract from "Sex and death lie at the poisoned heart of religion" by Polly Tonybee in *The Guardian* copyright © 2010, Polly Tonybee. Reprinted by permission of Guardian News & Media Ltd.
pp. 84: Extract from "British universities shouldn't condone this kind of gender segregation" by Polly Tonybee in *The Guardian* copyright © 2013, Polly Tonybee. Reprinted by permission of Guardian News and Media Ltd.

A catalogue record for this book is available from the British Library

Printed and bound in the UK, July 2015, LH26

To my ever supportive family: nuclear,

extended and church.

And to this imperfect yet wonderful country

in which we can discuss our disagreements

with openness and candour.

Contents

Acknowledgments   9

Preface   11

Introduction: Who Says the Church is Dying?   13

1. Green Shoots   27

2. There's Life in the Old Dogs Yet   41

3. Squaring the Circle: Understanding the Figures   55

4. The Church in Public Life   73

5. Service and Power   95

6. Religion and Violence   109

7. Who is the Enemy of Progress?   123

8. Re-embracing the Church   143

9. A Change of Perspective   163

Notes   173

Acknowledgments

This book owes a huge debt of gratitude to a number of people, not the least of which are Tony at Lion Hudson and his able co-editor Richard.

There have also been countless little conversations with friends, experts, and expert friends who have helped shape my thoughts into some kind of coherent form. Their assistance has been uniformly invaluable, and any mistakes that you might spot in this text are entirely my fault and not theirs.

Preface

When I remarked to one my friends at church that I was writing this book, he quipped that it would likely be short.

Of course he was right in one respect: this is a comparatively short book; but his remark only spurred me on, because it highlighted the sense of hopelessness and cynicism that has settled in some parts of the church in the UK (as well as other parts of the Western world). It spoke of a grim fatalism about the way so many believe the church is going – a kind of "gallows humour" from the condemned.

Moreover it worried me, because it highlighted the fact that the narrative of decline that is the focus of this book had obviously infected the church as well.

For enemies of the church this will be welcome news of course, but they too need to read on; for the book concerns itself not simply with errors in this picture of church decline, but with full appreciation for the valuable work the church is doing quietly in every corner of the country. It is written in the hope that, in redressing the severely lopsided image we have of the church, we will be able to take a more informed view of what is really happening and of the value it brings to the life of the nation.

Nobody knows what is going to happen to the church in the UK: lots of people try to make projections and predictions – as they do about any subject – but this book is written in the belief that we need to rethink some of our current assumptions. Maybe then we shall re-evaluate what we think about the place of the church in modern, changing Britain. If this book achieves even that much, then it will have fulfilled its purpose.

Who Says the Church is Dying?

This book argues that elements of the "new establishment" are seeking to present a picture of Christianity in terminal decline in Britain, and that they do this for three specific purposes.[1]

What is this "new establishment"? As Simon Kuper describes in his article for the *Financial Times*, the new establishment is an elite that has developed outside of old class structures (although it still owes much to an Oxbridge education). It is an elite based on intellectual ability and an adherence to certain common perceptions, centred around London, that you can become a member of if, as Kuper describes, "you are clever and behave yourself". What does "behaving yourself" entail? According to Kuper it centres around an attitude that members are "discouraged from holding strong fixed beliefs. Literally anyone can be accommodated: 'God Save the Queen' by the Sex Pistols, the ultimate anti-establishment song, was played at the Olympic opening ceremony just before the Queen's own comic caper." Yet, this apparent openness conceals an important blind spot: they are vehemently opposed to the manifestation of any kind of religion. We will come back to the roots of this attitude in Chapter 4, but for the moment it's important to highlight this characteristic in relation to defining the group being labelled as "new establishment".

First, it allows this "new establishment" an excuse to avoid discussing religion as much as possible, other than in negative terms (such as abuse by priests and Islamic terrorism). The ultimate goal of this negativity is to encourage religion towards a quiet death. We shall consider the motives for this in Chapter 4, where we analyse the impact that the historical struggle between church and state has had on the mindset of the modern political class.

Secondly, in encouraging the death of religion they are being philanthropic for society at large. There is a belief among the "new establishment" that religion has been the principal cause of conflict throughout history, and so in aiding "the death of religion" they believe they are actually benefitting humanity.

Thirdly – and I believe this is the main motivation – the continued survival of religion is anathema to the Marxist narrative of history that we all seem to have swallowed whole. It is a narrative which tells us that humanity has been in continual progression throughout its existence; religion, which is equated with superstition, is eroded as "enlightened thought" (science) breaks the hold of religion over a fearful and ignorant populous. This worldview is the essence of the original *Star Trek* vision of humanity, in which religion is rejected as another superstition.

In politics this movement of enlightenment is frequently expressed as "progress". This aids the classification of those who might have an objection to change for change's sake as "dinosaurs" – the term used by the former British Liberal Democrat leader Nick Clegg to describe those who had qualms about the redefinition of marriage in the Marriage (Same Sex Couples) Act 2013.[2]

So in this book I shall try to correct misconceptions about the decline of Christianity and expose the agenda which drives those misconceptions. I hope not only to expose a myth which seems to have become a fact, but also to encourage Christians in Britain to take heart and to keep going.

It's a church that could certainly do with the encouragement of a positive message about both its vitality and its contribution to society, for one of the most tragic aspects of the impact of the "decline narrative" is that the church itself seems to have bought into it. The Right Reverend Tim Thornton, Bishop of Truro, was quoted in 2014 as saying that the Church of England will struggle to exist in ten years' time.[3] Sadly, Bishop Thornton's morose prediction appears to be borne out in the numbers we are seeing in polls and censuses.

Census data

In 2001 the optional question of religious belief was added to the UK census for the first time since 1851. It reported that 37.2 million people had chosen to call themselves

Christians – a figure that equates to about 71% of the population. When the same question was included in the 2011 census, the number had dropped to 33.2 million – 59.3% of the total population.[4]

This was a substantial drop, but it was pointed out by the Christian think-tank Theos at the time of the 2011 census that the question was voluntary. And it was right at the end of the survey among the identity questions. Furthermore, the option to tick "Christianity" was below that of "No Religion". It is therefore not surprising that 7.2 million people chose not to answer the question: a number that is significant enough to have made quite a difference to the results.

But whatever the quibbles about the style or wording of the questions, the figures from the censuses seem clear enough: fewer people were self-identifying as Christians. What's more, the findings were in line with a Parliamentary report on social indicators on religion in general, which concluded that there were around 570,000 fewer Christians year on year between 2004 and 2010.[5] These findings confirmed one element of the report on Christian decline in the West that was published by Pew, the highly respected Washington-based think-tank in 2013.[6] The report highlighted that in 1900 some 80% of the world's Christians lived in Europe, but by 2005 that had fallen to 40% and was projected to fall to just 30% by 2050.

Religious polls

These findings are given further weight by the data collected in various polls on attitudes to religion and spirituality conducted in the UK over a number of years.

For example, the Conservative party peer, Lord Ashcroft, conducts regular polling on lots of different social attitudes across the UK, and his large sample (8,000) was asked in November 2013 about their membership of religious groups or bodies. Over a third (38%) said they had no religion. Lord Ashcroft's findings (Populus did the actual polling) matched the findings of two YouGov polls that were taken in December 2013 in preparation for the ongoing Westminster Faith Debates. These numbers suggested a growing atheist trend, especially when we see that those citing "no religion" were actually in the majority (51%) for the 18–24 year-olds in Ashcroft's survey, and nearly a half (44%) of the 25–34 year-olds, suggesting a continuing journey of secularization along successive generations.[7]

These recent surveys are backed up by academic research over a number of years, which has also tracked a downward trend in religious affiliation (of any kind). For example, the Labour Force Survey asked questions about beliefs in both 2004 and 2010. In 2004, 15.7% of respondents selected "no religion"; in 2010 that figure had risen to 22.4%. The numbers in the British Social Attitudes Surveys of 2001 and 2009 were even more clear in the picture they presented: 41.2% of those surveyed chose "no religion" in 2001, rising to 50.7% in 2009.[8]

We recognize, of course, that surveys are not identical in their approach, and one of the reasons for the difference between the findings could lie in the different questions that were asked. For example, the Labour Force Survey asked, "What is your religion, even if you are not currently practising?", whereas the British Social Attitudes Survey asked, "Do you regard yourself as belonging to any particular religion?" Of course, the questions drive at the same outcome, but whereas the Labour Force Survey question allowed people to think about their spirituality in a more open-ended way, the British Social Attitudes Survey directed them towards institutional religion. It is therefore likely that the British Social Attitudes Survey was, at least partly, a comment on the lack of attachment to institutional faith, rather than an express rejection of the notion of God. And that is important.

Even so, both these surveys, and the 2006 ICM poll for the *Guardian* newspaper (which showed 26% of respondents having "no religion"), certainly continued the narrative of decline which we have seen in the other polls.[9]

Church surveys

It's not just polls from non-religious organizations that would have us believe that the church is in terminal decline in the UK and Europe.

Just look at the Tearfund survey on churchgoing published in 2007.[10] That report, which was based on a

7,000-strong survey pool, put the number of Christians in the UK far lower than the census in 2011 did, claiming that 53% of the total population were Christians. This depressing finding was all the more potent because it came from inside the "church body".

But leaving aside the figures for a moment, the observations of the analysts bear some reporting because, as already mentioned, they speak into a sense of relative hopelessness that has infected some parts of the church in the UK (indeed, the minority world more broadly). For in her introduction to the report Revd Lynda Barley, Head of Research & Statistics for the Church of England, declared gloomily that "we do not see people worshipping in our churches to any significant extent and growing numbers have lost touch with church in any shape or form". She added:

> *This Tearfund research helps us to understand that the further people are from the church (in terms of churchgoing), the less likely they are to attend in the future. Alongside this is the growing realisation that most people today see themselves as 'spiritual' rather than in any sense 'religious'.*

It is a vision of de-institutionalization and globalizing syncretic beliefs which point towards a decline of any kind of single believing identity.

Nor is the sense of doom confined to the Protestant part of the church. David Barrett of the *Catholic Herald* dolefully proclaimed that baptisms, ordinations, and marriages were all in decline according to the Catholic church's 2013 figures.[11] His article focused on the fact that the 1960s had been a high point for Catholic church attendance, but that things had been rather downhill since then.

Adding to the sense of inevitable death for Christianity in the UK, Peter Brierley, former head of Christian Research, addressed a conference of Pentecostal believers in May 2010 and quoted number after number that pointed in the same downward direction.[12] According to the conference report he "painted a harrowing picture of the decline in attendance across English counties in the last 12 years". Particularly significant were the attendance numbers Brierley quoted for those under twenty years old, and for those approaching middle age, both of whom seemed to be drifting away. He ended with a stark warning:

> *While Christianity is likely to continue declining, other religions in Britain will see growth, particularly Islam, with the number of Muslims expected to grow to 3 million by 2020... The problem is that the ministerial age matches the congregation but not the people they need to reach.*

Brierley's words are sobering for anyone who is interested in Christian participation in the life of Britain. And yet, around the same time as his and Tearfund's reports were published, the then editor of *The Economist* John Micklethwait and his Washington bureau chief Adrian Wooldridge were publishing their book *God is Back* (whose findings are discussed in the next chapter) which presented a different vision of the future. So a Catholic and an atheist were making predictions of a future that were somewhat less religion free than that of the Protestant evangelicals.

But despite Mickelthwait and Wooldridge's encouraging words, the truth of Brierley's dire predictions seemed to have been confirmed in March 2014 when the *Daily Mail* pushed a story citing new estimates that put the total number of Church of England attendees at about 800,000. The story also highlighted that the number was less than half of what it was in the 1960s and that, furthermore, it was part of a broader decline in Christian faith generally.[13]

So in this book I hope not just to highlight the barely noticed changes in church attendance which are creating a groundswell across the country, but also to stop the juggernaut of "decline narrative" from flattening the morale of a church that is doing vital work, in all kinds of ways, across the UK.

In order to do that the next few chapters will explore and refute the claims of decline by analysing the numbers for and against the "decline narrative". The second part of the book will turn from the numbers to the motivations behind the decline narrative that has taken root. This will bring us to the final chapters which will discusses the outworkings of a more informed view about Christianity in Britain.

Of course, this is not the only book to wade into these stormy waters. Over the last few years, particularly since the advent of the 9/11 and 7/7 atrocities, religion has rarely been out of the news. But while many books have looked at Islam in relation to the changing face of Europe, far fewer have sought to evaluate the place of Christianity in Britain, or to challenge current received wisdom about the decline of Christianity.

Recent literature

The book which is perhaps closest to this one in terms of subject matter is *Church Growth in Britain* (2012), edited by the Durham University scholar David Goodhew. It is a series of essays that explore the truth behind the facts and figures we see concerning the health of the church. Not surprisingly it has been a very useful source, as I have sought to find out the reasons behind why church growth is not being reported. The work of David Goodhew and his co-authors has made my task much easier.

Another important book I acknowledge a debt to is Micklethwait and Wooldridge's *God is Back*, subtitled "How the Rise of Faith is Changing the World" (2007). This is a book whose rigorous research, sharp analysis, valuable insights, and fearlessness in speaking up for what could be seen as unpopular opinions have been immensely encouraging to me. *God is Back* was global in scope and had relatively little on Britain (or continental Europe), as its primary focus was the impact of Christian growth in Africa and Asia, but their citation of the little glimmers of growth that they spotted back in the mid-noughties became the foundation (along with *Church Growth in Britain*) on which Chapter 1 is built.

Another popular work, this time by the US academic Philip Jenkins, is *God's Continent*. This book specifically compares the places of Christianity and Islam on the religious map of Europe. Jenkins' main interest is in trying to understand the impact of Muslim immigration to the continent, from both a religious and broader cultural perspective. His excellent book contains a lot of very useful figures and observations, to which my book owes a debt of gratitude. However, we shall be exploring a different field from that which Jenkins surveyed, and shall be adding new data unavailable to Jenkins when he was writing.

Next, I am indebted to a tragically little-known article by the journalist and author Jenny Taylor, which is based on her PhD research, called "After Secularism: Inner City Governance and the New Religious Discourse". It was later included in a volume edited by the highly respected sociologist of religion Professor Grace Davie of Exeter University. It was written back in the mid-1990s, yet even at that time it spotted the emerging trends which we will get to later – almost fifteen years before many of those mentioned in this book began to take note of them.

There are a number of prominent "new atheists" in this dialogue, including the bestselling authors Richard Dawkins, Christopher Hitchens, and Sam Harris. But one of the big pieces of writing engaged with in this book is Callum

Brown's *The Death of Christian Britain, Understanding Secularisation 1800–2000* (2009) where he argues that British Christianity experienced a rapid, catastrophic decline over the course of the last two centuries. Brown's work has therefore been an invaluable source upon which to think about the counter-arguments which form the core of this book.

Closer though to the perspectives in this book are the set of essays found in *Re-Defining Christian Britain: Post-1945 Perspectives* (2011), which brings together a distinguished set of scholars to analyse the impact of Christianity on many differing aspects of British culture, from politics to art and beyond. The observations of Jane Garnett and her colleagues have been very helpful in thinking through the direction of this book. The same must be said for Nick Spencer's *Freedom and Order: History, Politics and the English Bible* (2011).

In 2005 Jim Wallis's bestselling *God's Politics* ("How the Right got it wrong and the Left doesn't get it") explored the way that Christianity gets used (and sometimes abused) on the political scene. Wallis was focused on American politics and on the principles that should underpin religion in public policy, but his observations were certainly pertinent on the opposite side of the Atlantic as well. I shall not be engaging with the theology of politics in the same way. Instead I shall be trying to debunk the myths and challenge the assumptions about Christianity in the UK which seem to have become so ingrained that even the church itself seems to believe them.

It is important that these perceptions are challenged, not only for the sake of accuracy, but also so that all of us – whatever we think of faith or Christianity or religion in general – can consider the place of the church in public life with both eyes open, rather than only one. For, if current misconceptions are left unchallenged, politicians are more likely to enact policies which take no account of Christian perspectives that will be deemed irrelevant or altogether redundant. Furthermore, I hope that challenging the negativism and the narrative of decline will encourage the wider, non-churchgoing public to think about whether the end of the church in the UK is really so desirable.

CHAPTER 1

Green Shoots

In this chapter we'll look at the body of data which paints a very different picture of church vitality, and explain why there is good reason to believe that the church in Britain will grow in the years to come. Useful sources of data will be those available on the impact of "Fresh Expressions", *Quadrant* from the Christian Research Institute, as well as the excellent work done by Eric Kaufmann at UCL. As we wend our way over the mountain of data, we'll be driving towards a question: "If this is really what's happening, then why is it not being acknowledged?" That will become the pivot around which we'll move from dealing with the "real picture" to deconstructing the misrepresentations that lie behind the story of "decline" that we have heard so much about.

Not so splendid isolation

If ever there was a difficult task, then showing that the church in the UK is actually growing rather than declining has to rank as one of the most impossible of the lot. Even one of my sons, who is a Christian himself, looked at me incredulously when I said to him that the church in the UK as a whole is actually increasing rather than declining. In reply he didn't come back at me with figures; he simply gave me an anecdote from his own life. It was one that is almost certainly repeated all over the country. He said, "At college, I'm pretty sure that I'm the only Christian. I mean, no one else I know even knows anything about the Bible, and they laugh at me if I talk about it."

This sense of isolation is perfectly natural. Over the past three years the Church of England has been conducting some extensive research on the reasons for growth or decline in church attendance. Some of its findings are expected, such as the fact that areas of growth are generally those which have a church leadership with vision and a congregation which is keen to look outside its own walls.[1] But, in the executive summary of the report, the authors make it clear that there is a real problem with successive generations becoming more and more "secular".

My son's experience would therefore seem increasingly to be the norm. The recent report from the Anglican Research and Statistics unit bears out his observation, for in the summary of their findings they argued:

> *The reason for decline in affiliation and attendance is the failure to replace older generations of churchgoers. The problem is not adults leaving the Church: it is that half of the children of churchgoing parents do not attend when they reach adulthood.*[2]

All this provides fuel for the notion that the church in the UK really is in decline.

A light in the darkness

A report came out in 2013 by the Parliamentary Research Service which showed in clear figures that the decline that had been reported up to the 2011 census was being sharply reversed. In 2011 the Christian population of the UK had stood at 59.3%, whereas in the Parliamentary paper the Christian population was cited as 59.9%.[3] If we assume the accuracy of both figures, this means that in just two years the Christian population had risen by approximately 320,000 people. That is pretty astonishing growth for a two-year period. Put in perspective, it is the same as the entire population of Reading being added to the church within two years.

So is this reliable and if it is has this come out of the blue? Back in 2007 Wooldridge and Micklethwait's *God is Back* spoke of Europe's signs of life in the church. The research they cited is solid and extensive but, on the evidence of the Parliamentary paper, perhaps conservative and cautious.[4] Maybe, at the time they were writing, the signs were not that obvious. Certainly not many analysts were pointing out the shifts, which *God is Back* cited. We'll get into why so many have failed to acknowledge the change later in the book, but first we need to spend some time making sure that the findings of the Parliamentary paper, and Micklethwait and Wooldridge's observations, do have a solid foundation.

First of all, what did Mickelthwait and Wooldridge actually say? They reported that at least 2 million Britons had been on an Alpha course, and that these participants had had an average age of twenty-seven.[5] Secondly, the number of adult confirmations had risen (sharply). Thirdly, pilgrimages were "booming". And fourthly, immigration was making a substantial impact in two ways: the arrival of Muslim immigrants had made many "nominal Christians more aware of their spiritual inheritance"; and immigrant numbers contained a significant number of Christians themselves, many from Africa.[6]

Let's explore the truth of their claims.

Alpha males – and females

In March 2013, ten days after the enthronement of Justin Welby as Archbishop of Canterbury, the *Independent* newspaper ran an article about Alpha, the interactive course exploring Christianity developed by Nicky Gumbel, now Vicar of Holy Trinity Brompton church in central London.[7] The course is a series of typically ten sessions and tackles a different facet of Christian doctrine each week. There is a meal and the participants are encouraged to ask any questions they like. There is no charge.

The format has proved extraordinarily successful. Between 1993 (when the courses were first launched in their current format) and 2012 (the last year we have figures for) the total number of British participants was 3.3 million. There have been 21.1 million participants worldwide.[8]

By any measure this is significant. The course has consistently grown in popularity year on year (other than 2002 which showed a 1% decline). In fact figures for 2010–12 show that, year on year, 0.5% of the total British population attended an Alpha course. Of course we don't know how many of these attendees were new and how many were returners, but there can be little doubt that the course is making a positive impact.

Rising confirmations

So Micklethwait and Wooldridge seem to have a point about the impact of Alpha but what about confirmation? They used the phrase "risen sharply" when they described the increase in church confirmations and what makes this surprising is that, although all the denominations have some form of baptism, only the Church of England does confirmation – yet it is precisely this kind of traditional denomination that is seen as a principal "decliner". Might this be a small glimpse of church growth, without providing the kind of broad evidence that we could find in general population statistics? Certainly it would be worthwhile trying to see what Micklethwait and Wooldridge saw back in 2007, and check to see whether the trend has continued or changed.

On first glance, the evidence seems good. Gillan Scott highlighted the improvement in the number of confirmations within the Church of England on his *God and Politics in the UK* blog in 2013. He pointed out that "christenings are up 4.3%, adult baptisms are up 5%

and thanksgivings for the birth of a child posted an 11.9% increase".[9] This is certainly good news for Christians, but what about those confirmations? Scott had a graphic in his article which showed that between 2001 and 2011, male and female confirmations had risen by 2 and 3% respectively. Encouraging in many ways, but hardly explosive. Furthermore, the story wasn't all about growth. Scott's article also showed that all the groups under nineteen years of age had either remained at their previous levels, or declined slightly. So it was a picture of "fizzle" rather than "sharp rises".

Maybe it was the baptisms that were providing the incline described in *God is Back*?

Perhaps, but what do these figures really mean when we start digging? Maybe, rather than evidencing a growing church, it points to some British people seeking their "spiritual heritage", as Wooldridge and Micklethwait also observed. Of course, it doesn't have to be one or the other, it might be a combination of both; but, whatever the truth, using confirmations as an evidence of Christian growth seems to be the most contestable element of the case. That's not to say it is useless, but instead to say that it probably doesn't help the case for growth as much as some of the other elements we're looking at.

Pilgrim fathers and mothers

So confirmation numbers seem to be a somewhat shaky source of evidence for growth. But what about "booming" pilgrimages? The lady in the white-and-pink-striped shirt in front of me was chatting away as we walked the final 150 yards down the narrow streets, with their distinctive Norfolk pebbled houses, towards the Church of Our Lady of Walsingham. Others were silent, like the older well-dressed man to my left who didn't seem to be looking around very much, so focused was he on arriving at our destination. Looking around me for the hundredth time that day, taking in the mixture of people that made up my travelling companions, I wondered what stories had brought them here to this point in their lives. I was conscious of a profound peace, for the first time in a long time, coupled with the familiar tingle of excitement that I always got when I felt a connection with history – especially history that also touched my faith; I remembered the same feeling when I had visited Ephesus with my family in the summer. In Walsingham, as in Ephesus, I thought about the many thousands who had trod the roads I had, and what had brought them there.

One way of measuring the growing popularity of pilgrimages is, perhaps, in the increasing number of books on the subject. In 2011, for instance, the Church of England published a *Pocket Book of Prayers for Pilgrims*.[10] However, we do not just have to rely on the marketing strategy of the Anglican Church to get evidence of such growth.

In 2009 Dr Ian Bradley, a Reader at the University of St Andrews, wrote *Pilgrimage: A Spiritual and Cultural Journey*.[11] The book is a mixture of descriptions and facts about Christian pilgrimage in the modern era. In an interview with the *Daily Telegraph* newspaper Dr Bradley observed that "pilgrimage is enjoying a huge revival across Europe". He went on to say, "While figures for churchgoing continue to fall across Europe, the number of those making pilgrimages is steadily rising. Many people uncomfortable about sitting in pews and uneasy with institutionalized religion find it easier to walk rather than talk their faith."[12]

Dr Bradley's comments on church decline aside, his observations about the rising popularity of pilgrimage are supported not only by a good deal of solid evidence in his own book but also by statistics found at other research portals. The Alliance of Religions and Conservation (ARC), for example, lists the most popular sites for pilgrimage every year.[13] These include many internationally renowned non-Christian sites, such as the estimated 30 million who travel to Amritsar, Tirupati and Ayyappan Saranam in India, and the Arba'een at Karbala in Iraq. But included in the ARC list is Iona, which it cites as receiving 250,000 pilgrims, Walsingham as receiving 100,000 (as compared to 16,500 in 1970) and St Albans as receiving 2,500 pilgrims per year. These are very small numbers when compared to the 1 million who visit the Church of the Holy Sepulchre in Jerusalem or the 4 million who go to Lourdes. But they still represent a six-fold increase over the numbers back in the 1970s.

As both Ian Bradley and author Peter Stanford suggest, it may be that the growth of pilgrimage as a spiritual pursuit could be part of a wider desire to move away from structured services, and move towards an active spiritual journey instead.[14]

The key pilgrimage sites in the UK are generally Roman Catholic (although Iona is not), so we might expect this upsurge in pilgrimages to have a knock-on effect in turnout at Catholic services. Not so. It isn't that Catholic numbers are falling – they have held up well, as have other historic orthodox branches of the Christian church. However, the rapidly growing numbers of pilgrims do not seem to be taking their physical and spiritual journeys into new membership of the Catholic Church itself. According to the research website Christian Research, the Roman Catholic Church in the UK was growing until 1960, when it began to decline. However, since 2005 the numbers have broadly stabilized.

Some people have put this down to Polish immigration. There is no doubt that many Eastern Europeans have been attending mass in the UK, but, as Christian Research went on to point out, if this had been the sole reason for Catholic number stabilization then we would have expected to see the numbers fall again very quickly when the economic downturn caused many Poles to return to their homeland. That wasn't the case.[15] Moreover, as David Barrett pointed out, there has been an overall increase in membership of the Catholic Church in the UK as the number of members has risen from 1.8 million in 1912 to 4 million in 2010.[16] Of course, the population as a whole has also risen hugely in that time, so it seems that the Catholic Church has basically kept its proportion of the population the same throughout the century – something it has done worldwide.

Lastly, there has been a small but noticeable increase in the number of people going for a monastic life. The numbers are tiny (thirty men and twenty-three women in 2012, up from nineteen and six in 2009) but the growing numbers are undeniable.

So the Catholic Church could be said to be holding its own. Catholicism has not seen the spectacular success of the Pentecostal movement (which we'll turn to in a moment), but equally it shows no signs of terminal velocity and the growing numbers of pilgrims might indeed begin to translate into growing church attendance.

The impact of immigration

Go to London on any given late Sunday morning, particularly the boroughs of Southall, Southwark, or Stoke Newington, and you are likely to meet groups of richly attired Africans clustered on the pavement chatting at the entrance to a former pub or cinema. They have just held a church service in there.

For the indigenous population (however that is defined) "immigration" has become a word which has sown fear into the hearts of many. In fact, such is its fear-factor that it has rated as one of the key issues in political campaigns since 2010. Change is uncomfortable, and the sense that the place that we called home is now so different that we might not even think to call it home any more feels like a fundamental attack on our security – even our identity. Migration into the UK, in common with the rest of the developed world, has been alarming for some precisely because they no longer recognize the place that they call home.

Some of the fear has been encapsulated in concern about Islam, borne out of the images we see on our TV screens, or in the concentrated communities in many of our cities, such as East London, Bradford, and Birmingham. Of course, one of the things that the official censuses have shown, other than Christian decline, is Muslim growth. This toxic combination of shrinking numbers of institutionally affiliated Christians and a concurrent rise of sometimes hostile beliefs unsurprisingly results in fear.

Yet what is generally forgotten or ignored in this culture of creeping dread is that there have been far more Christian immigrants to the UK than Muslim (or any other belief). Back in 2009 the highly respected think-tank, IPPR (the Institute for Public Policy Research), published a report into the impact of immigration on faith. It concluded that, although one quarter of immigrants were Muslim, over half were Christian. Charismatic and Pentecostal churches had done particularly well.[17]

The impact of this Christian influx has been seen particularly in London, where the 2011 census figures themselves showed that Christians have increased by nearly half a million at the same time as the White population of the city has declined from 58% to 45% of the total. The boroughs of Hackney and Newham have seen the greatest increases. Among the most active and energetic of the new churches is KICC (the Kingsway International Christian Centre), founded by the Nigerian Pastor Matthew Ashimolowo, which was featured in a *Guardian* article in 2009. The article focused both on the success of its growing congregation and also the fact that it was the wealthiest single church in the UK.[18] Pastor Ashimolowo's church is not unique, and a survey commissioned by the London City Mission (and reported on the website of the National Secular Society) confirmed that churchgoing increased in London between 2005 and 2012 by 720,000 – driven, the article argued, by the impact of Pentecostalism.[19]

The University of Roehampton academic Andrew Rogers spent two years cataloguing and investigating the churches in the borough of Southwark, because he wanted to understand the dynamics behind a mounting problem with the unauthorized use of disused buildings as places of worship. In addition, as he explained in his introduction, Rogers wanted to research the truth of a comment he had heard, which had suggested that Southwark held a particular significance among Black Majority Churches (BMC), as it was the first area of London to have a recorded BMC back in 1906.[20] Rogers discovered that there were 240 churches in that borough alone, ranging from several hundred attendants to just a small group. Indeed, the heavy concentration of BMCs in the borough attracted the attention of the *Independent* newspaper, whose article focused on the fact that the borough is believed to be home to the greatest concentration of African churches outside of the continent itself.[21] Its impact on the church in the UK as a whole was not mentioned in the article.

This BMC growth has been tracked by the respected academic Eric Kaufman of Birkbeck College, University of London.

In 2006 Kaufman wrote:

> *My projections, based on demographic*
> *differences between the populations and*
> *current patterns of religious abandonment,*
> *suggest that the secular population will*
> *continue to grow at a decelerating rate*
> *for three or four more decades, to peak*
> *at around 55 per cent. The proportion of*
> *secular people will then begin to decline*
> *between 2035 and 2045 ... This slow shift*
> *against secularisation would have only a*
> *gradual impact on the spirit of European*
> *society were it not for immigration.*[22]

In the wake of the publication of the 2011 census, Kaufman highlighted the importance of London as a "looking-glass" through which to see the shape of the future.

> *These [census figures] show that the*
> *proportion of white British in the capital*
> *declined from 58 to 45 percent of London's*
> *population in ten years, twice the fall*
> *recorded in England. But hold on: the*
> *number of Christians nosedived by 3.8*
> *million in England but fell a mere 220,000*
> *in London ... In nine London boroughs, the*
> *number of Christians actually increased,*
> *with Hackney and Newham topping the*

list. Now let's add non-Christians to the picture. The number of religious people in England declined by over 2 million in the past decade but grew by 440,000 in London. In seven London boroughs, reverse secularisation took place. In Redbridge and Newham, the share of nonreligious people in the population was cut in half! This has ramifications for the religious geography of England. London, especially ethnically diverse boroughs like Newham and Redbridge, is where the faithful of England are congregating. Demography, in the form of immigration, religious fertility and a young age structure, is driving the shift. Several years ago, a study discovered that 60 percent of parishioners in London churches were nonwhite. Few were white British.[23]

So the impact of immigration has been a significant rise in the numbers of Pentecostal churches, as that is the preferred denomination of many BMCs, as well as the growth of African background congregants across all the Christian denominations.. But what of the Church of England and the other more traditional Christian denominations? Is church growth in the UK simply dependent on immigration?

CHAPTER 2

There's Life in the Old Dogs Yet

There was something very raw, very intimate about the tiny chapel service in a backstreet behind the town's main shopping district. The group had begun only three years earlier, meeting in the pastor's front room. Eight of them had been part of the local Methodist church two streets away. They believed that God was telling them to step away from that congregation of sixty-three, which had been the spiritual home to some of them for more than a decade, and go to somewhere new. The pastor of the fledgling flock, Mike, wasn't a charismatic man: he was not televangelist material, although he did have a strength of purpose hidden behind his glasses. But his faithful leadership had seen the group outgrow his front room, to the point that he decided to take over the lease on a recently closed clothes-shop to accommodate his growing congregation. And now I was sitting there on a Sunday morning, in a freshly re-carpeted shop, with the twenty other members of this new church.

The traditional denominations

This story is not as unusual in modern Britain as we might believe. The decline of Methodism in the capital (11%), as well as Anglicans (9%) and Baptists (9%), was cited in the same article that highlighted the growth of Pentecostalism. It is one of the central tenets of the "decline narrative" that the rapid decline among older denominations is symptomatic of a general decline in Christianity across the UK. We've seen that Pentecostalism especially belies that narrative; but what about these older denominations themselves?

Over a number of years the Fresh Expressions movement within the Anglican Church has on average been doubling, nearly tripling, the numbers of its first attendees in thousands of tiny house-churches around the UK. The research unit of the Church Army carried out an extensive survey involving 518 church leaders over ten dioceses between 2012 and 2013. They found that nearly half (44%) of the churches they surveyed began after 2010. Furthermore, the statisticians worked out that approximately one-third of the members could be described as previously "de-churched", and a further half were non-churched.[1]

This Church Army survey finding was confirmed in the findings of the Research and Statistics Department of the Archbishop's Council. Their *Statistics for Mission 2012* report (the most recent one available) was based on the data collected from 85% of the Church of England parishes.[2] The report contained one diagram which showed the number of joiners and leavers according to the reasons for either. Fascinatingly it showed that of the 50,309 people that were reported to have left the church, 12,250 walked away completely; the rest either died or were too ill to go to church (19,484) or moved somewhere else. On the other side, 71,476 were reported as joining the church. Clearly that included many of those who had moved from somewhere else (22,773). But if we leave them to one side for a moment, the report's incredible finding was that 38,225 people came to church for the first time in 2012, and a further 10,478 returned to church after a period away.

This means that the number of people that either went to church for the first time, or returned to church after some time away, far outstripped those that had left. Indeed, if we bear in mind that those who died had no choice about whether they went to church or not, then the number of people coming to church as compared to the number leaving makes church growth in the Church of England look pretty healthy.

The numbers of those joining and those leaving make for only part of the picture. The same report also showed that the number of churches showing declines (23%) was slightly greater than those showing growth (20%).

So how do we square the circle?

One obvious answer is that the reported decline in numbers must at least in part be based upon the death and infirmity of older congregants. That can't be helped. But given that the number of people actually rejecting faith is relatively small year on year, especially as compared to those coming to the church (either for the first time or as returners), it makes the whole argument about "growing secularization" look rather weak. And that's if you focus on the Church of England, let alone include the growth talked about among other Christian denominations or, indeed, other faiths.

So there is reason to believe that the Church of England is growing, especially if we cut out those who have died and therefore have no choice in the matter.

But what about the other traditional Protestant churches – the Methodists, Baptists, and Brethren? Are the statistics of doom and gloom accurate here?

The Methodist Church prepared a very detailed report on their membership and attendance, which was published at their conference in October 2014. Their report *Statistics for Mission* was based upon data received from nearly all (99%) of their congregations.[3] Those figures did not reflect the growth seen in the Church of England, as they showed a reduction of 32% over the course of the last decade.

Clearly this figure did not reflect the narrative of growth that this chapter has been telling, but, digging below the surface, there were nevertheless some causes for encouragement. For example, in a graph below the headline numbers we've just mentioned, there was a more detailed breakdown of the story. They showed that, for every sixteen deaths, there were also seven new members. Furthermore, for every ten transfers out of the Methodist Church, there were a further eight transfers in. Presumably these were Methodists moving.[4]

Once again, death cannot be counted in relation to whether people are rejecting Methodism or Christianity as a whole. The graph did also show, as the Church of England graph had shown, that there were a number of former congregants who had simply "ceased to meet". However, unlike the Church of England numbers, there was no corresponding figure for completely new attendees. So, while the report highlighted a slow-down in the rate at which people were leaving, the figures still showed an overall decline.

For the Baptists the story of the last two decades and more has been mixed. As Ian Randall observed in his chapter dealing with Baptist church growth in David Goodhew's book, it seems clear that the number of Baptist *members* has fallen, yet there has been growth in the numbers *attending* services.[5] It is difficult to interpret from this whether we are witnessing growth in actual belief or simply spiritual searching. However, Randall spends a number of pages detailing spectacular Baptist growth in many different parts of the UK, both among indigenous communities and immigrant ones. For example, he cites the growth in the West Norwood Baptist Fellowship which doubled its size and has continued to grow ever since the early 1990s. Ninety-five per cent of its congregation are of Ghanaian background.[6]

For Randall the key to this growth has been localism, where local leaders have changed the mindset of their congregations from a defensive one (which had marked the period of decline up to the 1990s) to a missional one. So, while membership continues to fall, attendance is on the rise. Moreover, it can't be denied that Baptist leaders have been some of the key members of the wider "evangelical" revival movements that this chapter has already discussed. So it may very well be that, while denominationalism is on the decline among Baptists (as is institutionalism generally), they are playing a very full part in the wider growth of Christianity in the UK.

There can be little doubt that the Brethren movement has seen falls in membership over the last half a century. The decline does not appear to be letting up either. The movement is generally quite private, and so finding accurate figures to try to evidence growth or decline is difficult. That said, there was a report entitled *The "Brethren" Movement – a Briefing Note* in 2013 which was researched jointly by the Church Growth Trust and the Brethren movement's own Partnership based in Tiverton.[7] The report suggests that there are probably some 66,000 members across the differing Brethren denominations and it acknowledged that this figure represented a decline. Of course, many Brethren have been very influential in the evangelical Christian movement as a whole, including Billy Graham and a number of academics; so measuring Brethren numbers as a distinct group perhaps misses the point, and it might be fairer to include them among the growing ranks of the evangelical movement more broadly.

Scotland

So the picture to the south of the Tweed is quite mixed. Growth and decline are not confined to any one of the denominations, unless we are looking in the direction of (respectively) the Pentecostal Church or conversely the Methodists. But what about the church in the rest of the UK?

Unfortunately, it has to be said that the evidence does not look promising. In the 2011 census (out of a total population of 5,295,403) about half of Scots (54%) identified themselves as "Christian" – a drop of 11% from the last census in 2001. Of these a total of 1.7 million responded by saying that they belonged to the Church of Scotland, while a further 841,053 self-identified as Roman Catholics. The Church of Scotland figure was a drop of 500,000 whereas the Catholic numbers had increased slightly (by about 40,000). But beneath these headline numbers there were many interesting if complex dynamics. For example, those identifying as what the census defines as "Other Christian" included Church of England (67,000) and Pentecostals (12,357) as well as 36,000 identifying themselves as "Christian". Another 16,609 identified themselves as "Protestant" and a further 13,000 referred to themselves as "Evangelical".[8] So, on the face of it, the numbers for decline were pretty uniform across the board. Indeed, unlike in England and Wales, not even the Pentecostal or evangelical element of the church evidenced growth.

As Kenneth Roxburgh wrote:

> *The twentieth century has not been kind to*
> *Christianity in Scotland. A country which*
> *has been marked by significant levels of*

*Church and Sunday school attendance
has, since the 1960s, experienced a steep
decline...* [9]

Yet, for all that, Roxburgh also saw signs of growth, particularly in Edinburgh, which he outlined in a series of case studies. Among these growing churches was Morningside Baptist Church which had grown from 342 members in 1990 to 700 by 2011.[10]

So maybe there are not even "green shoots of recovery" as yet in Scotland, but what we can say is that there are signs of life which, to use an economic analogy, might become the platform for a broader-based recovery.

Northern Ireland

Here the identity of religion in relation to community identity is particularly strong. The 2011 census showed that Roman Catholics constituted 41% of the total population; Presbyterians were at 19%; the Church of Ireland at 14%; and Methodists were at 3%. For the Catholics, this represented an increase of just over 2% from 1991, while for the Protestant denominations there had been falls between 1991 and 2011 of 2% for the Presbyterians, 3% for the Church of Ireland, and 0.8% for the Methodists.[11] Not included, however, were figures for evangelicalism which is spread across the traditional denominations, especially the Presbyterians and the Baptists; and these do appear to be growing.

According to Claire Mitchell, "Rumours of Northern Ireland's secularization have been greatly exaggerated." She adds:

> *Whilst recent social and political changes*
> *in the region have been transformational,*
> *religion in Northern Ireland is interesting*
> *for its persistence as much for its change.*
> *This is particularly the case for evangelical,*
> *or born-again, Protestantism in Northern*
> *Ireland, which has demonstrated a*
> *remarkable capacity for adaptation.*[12]

Her chapter demonstrates these adaptations by exploring evangelicalism in the public arena, as well as looking at reasons why some are converting to Christianity. Many of the examples she cites seem to be relatively unconnected to each other, especially when discussing the rise in the "Morality Agenda" and "Liberal Evangelicals". Yet, as her conclusions articulate, the key to evangelical growth appears to lie in its engagement with modern culture, as well as its flexibility to adapt to the needs around it.

So the picture in Northern Ireland appears to be one of changing religious identities rather than growth itself. We could characterize it as a shift towards a "renewal" of faith as some new churches are created and, perhaps more directly, as traditional denominations are increasingly filled with evangelically orientated Christians.

Energetic Orthodoxy

Studies on church attendance by Christian Research show that the Roman Catholic Church, and indeed smaller Orthodox churches such as the Greek Orthodox and Coptic Church, have remained broadly stable in their attendance.

Some of this has been the direct result of the persecution of Christians taking place in areas where there had previously been moderately peaceful co-existence between Christians and other religious majorities. For example, the Allied interventions in Iraq and in Libya have been generally disastrous for the Orthodox Christian populations of those regions, as Islamist militants have set about claiming territory and persecuting Christian and other minorities in the region. Seeing the way the wind is blowing, many Christians have fled to other countries, including the UK, and this has boosted the numbers of Orthodox Christians living in the UK.[13]

An article published on the website of the Russian Orthodox Community in Gloucester and the Cotswolds on 4th July 2012 cited a number of figures for the growth and decline of various Christian traditions. Amongst them, it cited a figure of 63% growth for the Orthodox Church. This is a substantial number and, whether the number itself is entirely reliable or not, it does highlight what appears to be a clear upward trend.

The pillars of the earth

So there are many stories of growth, even vitality, across the Christian denominational spectrum, much of it captured (if only momentarily) by Micklethwait and Wooldridge. But there is one area they did not explore, and that is the growth of cathedral attendance. The Rector of St Michael's Cornhill in the City of London, Stephen Platten, had highlighted its growing importance a year before *God Is Back*, in 2006, in a book he had edited called *Dreaming Spires*.[14] In this series of essays contributors highlighted the unique contributions that cathedrals were increasingly making to the visibility of the church in the UK.

In highlighting the "publicity" significance of cathedrals, Platten's contributors seemed to be on to something. *The Pillars of the Earth* is Ken Follett's epic tale about the building of the fictional Kingsbridge Cathedral. Follett said that he became fascinated by cathedrals even before he began to research the book. His fascination stemmed from trying to understand one simple question: why did they want it?[15] We might question the extent to which medieval villagers or townsfolk did want it, but the question is still valid.

I'm sure we could think of all sorts of answers, but whatever the answer, the question itself points to the core reason why cathedrals are becoming increasingly used once again: they are visible and they connect us with the long story of Christianity in Britain that stretches back centuries. Cathedrals receive many thousands of visitors a year, most of whom may not necessarily be spiritually searching; but the very fact of coming into a cathedral and sensing a connection to the spiritual searchings of the past may indicate an empathetic connection with people whose questions are the same as ours, even though we are separated by centuries.

And then there are the congregations. An Open Research Business survey for the Association of English Cathedrals published in 2010 confirmed growing attendance at services. And while it found that 41% of all visitors throughout the week were attracted by the building, a further 10% came to find an opportunity to reflect.[16]

It may be that large, communal gatherings represent a desire to participate in something bigger. They offer time for spiritual reflection without the intimacy of a small service that might threaten your anonymity and force you to engage with people when you might just want time to reflect, or "dip your toe" in the water. Certainly this is what Professor Grace Davie of Exeter University highlighted when she suggested that the changing attitude to religion (combined with the impact of secularization) had moved people towards a consumer attitude towards faith, in which people went along to a service and had a spiritual experience, without necessarily making a commitment to attend the same church (or cathedral) on a regular basis.[17] This would fit with the trend we saw in denominations such as the Baptists we mentioned earlier, where church membership was down but attendance was up.

Seeing the wood for the trees

So have we managed to discover the source of that astonishing increase of 320,000 people I cited at the beginning of the last chapter?

Based on the evidence we've just been looking at, it seems pretty clear that something dramatic is happening in some parts of the church.

But is there decline or growth? Or is the answer a maddening "yes" to both? Or maybe an equally frustrating "it depends on how you look at it"!

How do we take the two diametrically opposed pictures we seem to have from these initial chapters and attempt to make any kind of sense of what we are seeing?

The next chapter will attempt to do just that. After that we can turn from fighting our way through the maelstrom of numbers and begin to investigate the agendas that lie behind the "decline narratives".

CHAPTER 3

Squaring the Circle: Understanding the Figures

In this chapter we'll be trying to understand why there are such diverging stories on church growth in the UK. To do this we shall need to drill down into some of the problems that exist with both the statistical models and the methods that are being used in the research. As we go through the various issues with the numbers on all sides, we'll get to a point where we can get a better sense of the "real picture". Then we can change tack and launch into the next part of the book, as we look at the agendas that lie behind the narratives we are being fed.

Trying to make sense of these figures is enough to give any academic, or reporter, a migraine: trying to understand whether one or the other narrative is true, or whether someone might be lying, or whether we should just give up trying to find out. It can be tempting simply to ignore whatever is happening; although if we do, we risk the maddening "maybe, maybe not, whatever works for you" syndrome. Yet that is not an option for this book. Nor indeed is it an option for anyone who wants to truly understand the trends and dynamics that lie behind the shifts taking place in modern Britain.

So, as we begin to unpack this perhaps it's best to be clear on what we do know. For instance, the data shows that the church is not some homogeneous mass, like a balloon, expanding inexorably in all directions at once. Instead, it's as if the balloon was suffering a kind of deformity, more like "the Blob", with some parts expanding really quickly while other parts don't. For while the overall story of the British church, according to the figures, seems to be one of growth, the lived experience for most Christians does not seem to back that up.

Maybe we should start by asking ourselves the awkward question: are these statistics really evidence of growth in the church, or are they simply an indication that there is spiritual searching going on – part of the wider quest for identity that's taking place all over the world? And is that search drawing people into seeking their spiritual heritage (as Wooldridge and Micklethwait highlighted) without necessarily coming to faith?

Much of what makes this question awkward is the fact that it is impossible to answer with total certainty without asking every person individually. Moreover, given the fact that all of us are on a journey in life, which will include the spiritual along with everything else, the same person may well give several different answers to that question throughout their life. Certainly that might account for the growth in church attendance while polls like Lord Ashcroft's give numbers that strongly suggest Christian belief is on the wane.

But I don't think that the data does suggest that. So let's go behind the numbers we've waded through, and try to get a sense of what we can really learn from them. What are the key dynamics that lie behind, and make sense of, the numbers?

A growth in "spirituality"

We'll begin by focusing on a study done in the far north of England.

The eminent expert on religious dynamics in the UK, Professor Linda Woodhead, was the lead researcher on a seminal study on religious trends in the Cumbrian town of Kendal. Kendal had been chosen as the object of the research because, statistically, its church attendance rate was slightly above the national average, but also because it appeared to be an important place for the new or alternative spiritualities as well.

Over the course of the study the two field researchers attended the twenty-six different churches around the town and the fifty groups which had been identified as "non-Christian". These included yoga classes, Buddhist meetings, reflexologists, homeopaths, and "sacred dancing" classes. The research included interviews with attendees at all the different religious activities.

The findings of Professor Woodhead's team pointed to the fact that people are not necessarily leaving the church for atheism, but that they are moving towards a general "spiritualness".[1] Professor Woodhead is by no means alone in this observation. A 2005 report on the anticipated shape of the world in 2020, by the highly regarded think-tank Chatham House, reported among its "mega trends" that adherence to religious institutions would probably break down and that, among the new "global middle class" in particular, a kind of universal spiritualness would replace specific doctrinal beliefs.[2]

And yet.

A decade on, the NIC (National Intelligence Council, who assisted with the Chatham House report) revised their opinion in their *Global Trends 2030*. For, where the earlier report had seen spiritual convergence, as had the EU's ESPAS report, the NIC now saw an increased international influence for international religious bodies (at the expense of state governments) through the call of loyalty they were able to make on their followers.

So what had changed the perceptions between 2005 and 2012?[3] Most likely, it has been a combination of a rapid rise in conversion (e.g. to Christianity in Africa and China) and a rise in nationalism, which has found expression in the growth of the nationalist parties in Europe, as well as in specific events such as the Scottish referendum and the Quebec independence movement. This renewed search for identity, the antithesis of globalization (even if it is a product of it), has created a twin-track dynamic in which greater global togetherness (through social media, online gaming, and ever faster transport) has also caused a fresh attempt to rediscover a sense of connection.

In a spiritual context, this globalized need to reconnect has led many not just through ethnic or cultural doors but through spiritual doors. In the UK, for some, this discovery of our spiritual heritage has meant literally walking through church doors, as they have reconnected with Christianity through visits to cathedrals (as we have seen). For others, however, it has meant an exploration of paganism and "new age" spirituality – as highlighted in the Kendal study we have already looked at.

Paganism and "new age" spirituality are particularly in evidence at historical re-enactments for ancient and Anglo-Saxon events, whereas Christianity has been seen more in events around the English Civil War, simply by virtue of the historical situation of Christianity in the country at that time. By way of example, every summer English Heritage has put on a history festival at Kelmarsh Hall in Northamptonshire. The event draws re-enactors from all periods of British history, with a large number of set-piece battles as well as smaller displays. There is a large tent village which includes a shopping area where the cash-rich punter can invest in specialist items such as medieval, Civil-War or Victorian clothing, swords, muskets, armour, pottery, and books. Prominent among the shops are a number of places which sell more "new age" or pagan items, including crystals, models, dragons, or rune stones. And this is repeated at medieval re-enactment events up and down the country.

So, for some at least, "spiritual openness" is connected to history and renewed cultural nationalism.

Everyone dies

As we dig down in our effort to reconcile these differing interpretations of the data, we pause to remind ourselves that the deaths which are cited as evidence of decline cannot be taken as a reasonable measure of the health of Christianity. If death (or serious illness preventing attendance) are removed from the data, the numbers look somewhat different. That is not to say that everything suddenly becomes rosy, but rather it helps us to correct the prescription on the lenses through which we are seeing the data.

The evangelicals are coming

The spectacular growth of the Pentecostal church, and the evangelical movement more broadly, cannot be denied; and, as Eric Kaufman has highlighted, it looks as though this trend is very likely to continue or even increase.

This fact was acknowledged by the acclaimed historian Simon Schama in a recent interview, where he is quoted as saying:

> *My generation grew up thinking that*
> *religion was completely marginal to British*
> *life, which, as for the rest of the world,*
> *has been proved more and more wrong.*
> *We were arrogantly isolated from that,*
> *thinking religion was just an ornamental*

> *part of Britishness. Now look at the success*
> *of the Alpha Evangelicals, how important*
> *Christianity has been to the community*
> *of West Indians, the huge place of Islam.*
> *Britain is becoming a more religious place,*
> *not less.*[4]

Leaving aside the discussions on the growth of Islam in the UK, which is a huge topic for a different book, Schama's words reflect a certain contrition, as well as bemusement. Both of these lead nicely into our discussion in the next chapters.

It's black and white

But first: how do we square the circle?

One very basic problem has been the "blind" spot that many who study the religious trends in the UK have when assessing church health: namely, a reliance on White indigenous data that ignores the growth in particularly Black Pentecostal churches. A classic example of this dynamic is the study we mentioned earlier, Professor Linda Woodhead's research on patterns of church attendance in Kendal. This project, researched between 2001 and 2003, has been very widely quoted in studies on church decline.[5] The problem is: they chose a White, middle-class town as the subject for study. As such, while the study could be said to be indicative of the spiritual life of White, middle-class Britain (especially with the ongoing fascination with yoga and far-eastern religion, as reported by Michaela Robinson-Tate[6]), it cannot be taken as a reasonable case-study for the general religious landscape of the country as a whole. For instance, if the study had been done on Southwark, the story would have been rather different.

The other problem with the Kendal study is that it is not age-specific.

It is apparent that there is a significant "cultural gap" emerging between the generations. As the Kendal study showed, there is a "bleed" taking place from church to "new age" or "mystic" faiths. My own sense, from being involved in inter-religious affairs, is that this "bleed" is taking place among those of the "baby boomer" generation, rather than uniformly across all generations. In other words, those most likely to be attracted to Eastern religions are those who spent their formative years at the time of the hippy revolution of the late 1960s and 1970s. For those of the X, Y, or millennial generations, Eastern religions do not seem to hold quite the same level of fascination. This could be because it has become more of a norm for their parents' generation, leading them to seek alternatives to something they didn't necessarily attach to themselves.

So where are people of those generations going now? Well, some of them at least are discovering Christianity, while others are finding Islam. In other words, they seem to be looking instead towards the monotheistic faiths, or at least those with some body of doctrine behind them, rather than the looser mysticism that was indicative of the spirit of the baby-boomer generation.

There is as yet very little raw data on this, but hints can be found in the Pew research quoted earlier. Hopefully, more concrete information will be forthcoming through the work of research being done at places such as the Center for Religion and Civic Culture at the University of Southern California.

But really, all of this is by way of saying there is a chance that the trend-mapping work has missed some important, subtle shifts which, if they are not spotted, could misrepresent what is actually taking place.

Changes over time

One other possible avenue of explanation perhaps lies in the passing of time. Many of the statistics quoted in the Introduction are earlier than those in Chapters 1 and 2. The Tearfund statistics, as well as many of the articles we quoted in Chapter 1, came in the early years of the century, while many of the growth figures come from the second decade. We might observe, then, that the current trend of church growth is very young.

This would not be an unreasonable explanation. However, it probably doesn't account for all the differences. After all, Wooldridge and Micklethwait published in the same year as the Tearfund survey, and they were able to spot signs of growth that Tearfund could not.

Another suggestion could be that, actually, the trend in both decline and ascent is not smooth, such that, in the years between the different sets of research, there are waves of sharper incline or decline. So the level of apparent increase or decline would depend on the particular moment that the poll was taken.

That is reasonable, if boring, but it doesn't really explain anything other than the obvious point that polling data is always subject to a certain degree of inaccuracy (although there is less chance of inaccuracy when a greater number of people are polled).

It is also true that statistics can prove most things, depending on the questions asked and the ways in which the data is sliced. The trouble is, that somewhat cynical viewpoint only serves to undermine the attempt to find an answer to any kind of survey. So it is probably best left alone, with the caveat that any top-line statistic needs to be investigated for the small print – a bit like picking your way through an insurance claim.

Wider cultural trends

If we move away from fixating on statistical interpretation, perhaps a better explanation of the growth we are seeing is to be found in our wider society.

Some might argue that the church is growing because people are finding solace in the face of the tragedies we see on the news. Others, perhaps, are retreating from the sexualization of society – even if this is not specific to Christianity: many (women particularly) have put their conversion to Islam down, in part, to their distaste for this aspect of society. Perhaps others simply want to step off the work treadmill and re-prioritize their lives away from selfishness and careerism towards service and simplicity. For example, in the quarterly *Wellness* survey that is carried out by the British Office for National Statistics, only 26.8% of respondents reported a very high life satisfaction (a 1.8% rise from the year before) and only 39.4% of respondents reported having very low anxiety the day before (a rise of 1.4% from the previous year). All of this confirms that there is both a general dissatisfaction and a high stress level present within the UK population.[7]

The desire to look towards the church for a new sense of life satisfaction might be partly due to the greater visibility of the church in national life (both positive and negative) through events as diverse as the royal wedding between the Duke and Duchess of Cambridge, the TV programme *Rev*, and the fierce debates over gay marriage and the place of women in the clergy. As the saying goes, "There is no such thing as bad publicity."

Maybe so. But this is rather a superficial explanation. Two further explanations seem to dive deeper and offer a more convincing explanation.

There is one explanation for the figures on church growth which is focused upon younger adults in the "millennial generation". Studies have shown that there is a general desire to attach to causes rather than simply be a member of an institution.[8] For example, a "millennial" might want to do something about the environment but will not necessarily join Greenpeace. So, for this generation, coming to Christian faith might not necessarily mean joining a specific church. Furthermore, the attachment to "cause" in faith terms might also explain the increasing radicalization among all faiths (such as Hindutva and Salafi or Jihadi Islam), for there can be little doubt that it is the moderate or "liberal" elements of faiths that are being eroded, leaving ground to the more literalist and scripturalist versions. This is true of Christianity also, where the evangelical movement has gained most of the ground.

Even more convincing by way of explanation are the findings of a study by Dr Roxane Gervais which were published at the Division of Occupational Psychology's annual conference in 2014. The small study (thirty-four) involved only people in full-time work and was a mixture of survey and interview. Her findings pointed to the fact that the demeanour and attitudes of Christians in work seemed to be favourably impacting their work-colleagues, to the extent that their interest is piqued enough to find out more and explore the faith for themselves. The study (from a secular organization) showed clearly that those with faith were far less likely to feel anxious, fatigued, or depressed at work. Moreover it found that "when their belief was cemented by regular church attendance, they tended to achieve an even bigger boost to their psychological constitution".[9] In a context where economic hardship is still current or fresh in the memory – not least for the millennial generation – such peace of mind would be even more attractive.

Faith in the land of the free

The Pew study on the "millennials" mentioned before was focused on the United States, although the attitudes found there seem to correlate with studies done in Europe. And since the US has been referenced, it would be worthwhile opening up the lens of our discussion for a moment to get a sense of whether these church dynamics in Britain are mirrored elsewhere in the "Christian heritage" world.

The US is a good foil because, like Britain, its past has been bound up with Christianity – and without the interruptions that characterize other nations. For example France, only 26 miles from the south-eastern tip of Britain, had a very sharp and deliberate separation from the church as part of its revolution. Numerous other countries – such as Spain, Italy, and Germany – had periods of dictatorship in which freedom to choose faith was heavily curtailed. So, even though the US has not had any established institutional connection with the church, there has been stable, democratic government as in the UK, and this has allowed relative freedom in religion for the last three centuries in both countries. So it is a fair comparison.

And it seems that, in the US too, there are stirrings among the huge churches that populate the vast, diverse United States of America – a country whose Christian populations had, until recently, seemed immune to the decline affecting their transatlantic cousins.

The total Christian population of the US, according to a poll taken by Gallup in 2012, is 77% – a clear drop from the

91% of 1948. But again in the US there are voices speaking of change, of vibrancy – even of church revival.

In October 2013 Ed Stetzer, the American author and church commentator, wrote an article in *Christianity Today* magazine in which he pointed out that to characterize the church in the US as "dying" was simply wrong.[10] He argued instead that it was in a period of transition.

On the face of it Stetzer's optimistic observations would be hard-pressed to find evidence. The *Huffington Post* was quick to get in a rejoinder: it carried a review of Ed Stetzer's article in October 2013 which attacked every part of Stetzer's argument, adding some damning statistics which seemed to evidence a rapid decline in the US church.[11] In the same book that spotted "green shoots of recovery" in Britain, Micklethwait and Wooldridge noted that as far back as 1968 Gallup published a poll in which 68% of Americans thought that religion was losing its impact on society. They argued that this loss of confidence among American evangelicals had been partly due to their "retreat from the public arena" following the Scopes Monkey Trial (in which a verdict incriminating a school teacher for teaching evolution was overturned), as well as the effects of Prohibition.

But it seems that Stetzer is not alone in his observations, for apart from him there has been a significant intervention from what could be seen as an unlikely source: Frank Newport, Editor-in-Chief of the very organization whose data tracked Christian decline – Gallup.

In the press release for his 2012 book *God is Alive and Well* Newport wrote:

> *It is possible that religion will be more*
> *significant in years ahead, and we may be*
> *on the cusp of a religious renaissance.*[12]

Now, let's not get ahead of ourselves. Newport was not singling out Christianity but including all religions, and there is no doubt that there has been significant growth for Mormons (birthrate and conversion), Muslims, and Hindus (birthrate and immigration) over the last three decades. Newport believes that "the votes of religious Americans may become the next major partisan battleground in American politics". He adds:

> *The Republican Party's monopoly on the*
> *loyalty of religious white Protestants has*
> *given it a highly motivated core of voters.*
> *This has in turn had a profound effect on*
> *American politics. That could change. The*
> *Democratic Party is increasingly aware*
> *of its weak positioning among religious*
> *Americans, and it knows it must "get*
> *religion" to win votes in the future.*

Furthermore, as *God is Back* also hinted, there are signs of specifically Christian revival happening in the US.[13] A July 2014 poll of 35,000 people for ABC News returned a result of 83% Christians. Among the sub-data that the poll tracked were some fascinating trends which seem to mirror that of Britain:

Evangelicalism soars particularly among blacks, and southerners: Two-thirds of blacks describe themselves as evangelical or born-again Christians, double the share of whites who do so.

Earlier in the same article the data showed that 37% of Americans were describing themselves as "Evangelicals". So it seems then that, in the US as in the UK, African Christianity is having a major impact on Christian revival. Furthermore, the growing numbers of Christians appear to be, in part, also due to the numbers of people choosing the faith but not a denomination. For many people who responded to the poll by categorizing themselves as "Protestant non-denominational" (19%), which suggests rapid growth among non-affiliated Free Churches, matching that trend in the Gallup surveys.[14]

Yet a 2009 poll for the "American Religious Identification Survey" of Trinity College in Hertford, Connecticut, reported by CNN, found that 75% of Americans called themselves Christian.[15] In 1990, according to the report, the number had been 85%. Even though that is a reduction, the figures are nuanced by understanding what William Donohue (President of the Catholic League) identified as a "radical shift toward individualism over the last quarter-century". He added: "Notice they are not Atheists – they are saying I don't want to be told what to do about my life."

His point is an important one and hints at that dynamic

we noted above about the "millennial generation". But that is not the focus of this book, so we will need to content ourselves with the acknowledgment that Trinity College's data shows a Christian decline in the US and look elsewhere for contrary evidence.

The results of a survey released by the Pew Research Center in October 2012 also confirmed the direction of travel observed by Gallup and Trinity College, although its data was slightly different in so far as it was exploring the rise of the "spiritual" rather than "religious".[16] The headline finding of their survey was that one-fifth of the American public and about one-third of adults under thirty described themselves as "religious unaffiliated". This meant that those describing themselves as "unaffiliated" had risen just under 5% over the previous five years. Of that number 6% described themselves as "Atheist or Agnostic", while 14% simply stated that they had no specific religious affiliation. This "Atheist or Agnostic" affiliation is much lower than in the UK and speaks to one of the many cultural differences between the transatlantic "cousins".

But whilst these surveys do show a downward trend, it is worthwhile noting that the ABC poll is more recent than any of the others. For that reason it may be that the US is seeing the same thing as the UK: that declines in the "noughties" are being reversed in the second decade of the century.

So there is a sense in which some of the confusion over numbers we have seen here in the UK, and possible explanations for the discrepancies are also being seen in the US.

Best-kept secret

Returning to the state of the church in the UK, it is likely that the reasons for the growth will be combinations of the explanations explored in these chapters, although it could conceivably be something entirely different. However, the bottom line (if official figures are to be believed) is that the church in the UK isn't just stopping the decline, it's growing – exponentially in parts.

That being the case, why isn't it being reported? Why isn't it item one on the news? After all, if the increase in numbers of California's Blue Whale population made it to the BBC website, why can't Christian growth numbers in the UK?[17]

CHAPTER 4

The Church in Public Life

It is time to move from the numbers to look at the possible motivations behind the lack of interest in reporting Christian growth. In this chapter and the next we'll be examining the first possible explanation, which is that ignoring the reality and telling a different narrative allows the "new establishment" an excuse to avoid discussing religion as much as possible, unless it is in relation to negative stories. Doing this enables people to buy into the notion that religion is a purely negative influence in the world and that the decline of religion is therefore something to be welcomed.

Why would they want to do that? To find an answer we'll look at some history. This will help us to understand the "long story" behind the agendas of those who would like to see the church die out. After we've explored that, we will turn to examining the basis of the negative perceptions themselves.

Church against state

Ever since the Middle Ages European states have had a somewhat turbulent relationship with religion in public life. At particular times the conflict has been open and frequently bloody.[1] Most of us will be familiar with the fights between the Tudor monarchs (especially Henry VIII and Elizabeth I) and the papacy, which culminated in the Spanish Armada of 1588. But we might not be so familiar with earlier squabbles which had taken place over much of western Europe and sometimes led to open war.

Take, for example, the struggles between Henry V, the Holy Roman Emperor, and Pope Paschal II. Henry insisted that he should have the right to give the bishops of Germany their offices, whereas the Pope argued that, as head of the church, it was his right alone. Paschal raised the stakes by publishing and renewing the decrees that stipulated popes alone could give bishops their posts. As both sides became more entrenched in their refusal to budge, there was an attempt to settle the issue through a meeting. However, that failed and, with no further prospect of compromise, Henry invaded Italy in 1110. The Pope, seeing the way the wind was blowing, suggested a compromise in which Henry would renounce his right to invest the bishops in exchange for the restoration of his right to rule the whole of Germany.

The problem was that this gift was not in the power of Paschal to give. So when Henry went to the Vatican to be crowned, the treaty was read out and was greeted with horror by the German nobility attending the coronation. The resulting wave of anger persuaded Paschal to refuse to crown Henry, whereupon Henry's soldiers seized Paschal himself and several of his cardinals. In the melee that ensued Henry was wounded, but he was still able to get away, taking Paschal with him. Perhaps unsurprisingly, the Pope changed his mind and crowned Henry after all.[2]

Farcical though this story is, it was deadly serious and was by no means the only spat between the medieval rulers and the popes.

Henry's clash with Paschal had been about the limits of royal authority, whereas Philip IV of France and Pope Boniface VIII clashed over Philip's drive to increase his coffers, which caused him to tax the French clergy (traditionally exempt) up to a half of their annual income. So incensed was Boniface that he issued *Clericis Iaicos*, a decree which forbade the French church from transferring any property to the monarchy. The protracted diplomatic battle which followed was only resolved when a new pope was elected who happened to be a French Archbishop (Bertrand de Goth) who, when he became Pope Clement V, promptly moved the papal court from the Vatican to the city of Avignon which was surrounded by French territory.[3]

However, significant though these incidents were, they pale in comparison with the greatest of the medieval struggles between monarch and church – those between Frederick II, Holy Roman Emperor, and a succession of popes, from Honorius III to Innocent IV.

Frederick succeeded in frustrating all these popes with a series of promises to go on crusade, none of which he honoured. Indeed, it got to the point, after defaulting on yet another promise in 1227, that Frederick was excommunicated by Pope Gregory IX. This was extreme by any standards, as the last resort of a pope to bring a "wayward" monarch back into line; but it was especially so when carried out against the Holy Roman Emperor himself, the very monarch who was meant to be the Pope's sword to punish other monarchs.

Frederick's insatiable territorial ambitions had constituted one of the primary causes of the conflict. Not going on crusade was just a symptom of the fact that Frederick was far more interested in developing his European power base than in helping the church. Even when he did finally sail for the Holy Land, he managed to get himself crowned King of Jerusalem by virtue of his marriage to Yolande, heir to the throne. At this point his territories were so immense, stretching from Sicily to Prussia, that the popes became seriously worried that he could become master of all Europe – a role they wished to keep for themselves. So when Innocent IV became Pope in 1243 he unleashed a propaganda and diplomatic war (which included financing Frederick's enemies in their rebellions) which eventually broke the Emperor.[4]

So this is just a flavour of the squabbles that wracked Europe through the Middle Ages.

But while the fight between church and monarch had seen victories for both sides at differing points, by the late fifteenth century, under the impact of the burgeoning Reformation, monarchs were increasingly able to take power away from the church to themselves. This was exemplified by the Tudor monarch Henry VIII who in 1537 managed to establish himself at the head of the new Anglican Church in order to take control over every sphere of his realm. In so doing he achieved a level of authority which had eluded his predecessors, most of whom had struggled with a church that was its own fiefdom.[5] Gradually, over a period of five hundred years, the public space was taken over by the state, at the expense of the church. By the time of the Enlightenment and the French Revolution, the church was being increasingly driven into the sphere of private belief. The seal was set on this state of affairs by the creation of the new state of Italy in 1865, which finally boxed the papacy into the Vatican City, removing the temporal power it had enjoyed as ruler of the Papal States.[6]

The early part of the same century had seen France's new emperor, Napoleon Bonaparte, strike a deal with the Papacy which defined the limits of Catholic engagement and Papal authority in the country. The Emperor's settlement provided the model for future French governments, for the law on religion that enshrined the famous principle of *laïcité* (passed in 1905) owed much to the principles established in the 1804 Concordat. Furthermore, in arriving at this settlement Bonaparte had stepped back from the more extreme anti-clerical elements that had characterized the earlier revolutionary settlement. So, although the Emperor was not interested in allowing the church back into the mainstream of public life again, he was also tacitly acknowledging that faith had a place in the life of state.[7]

But even in this headlong flight to clear the public space of religion, the fact that nation states came to agreements with the church, rather than seeking to completely destroy it, was an implicit acknowledgement of its social necessity. Although it is not hard to believe that, at the same time, they were hoping that its new-found lack of public space, coupled with pressure from the scientific revolution, might quietly kill it off.

Moreover, while there can be no doubt that the state wanted to be free from religious interference, that did not stop the rulers from using religion when it was useful to them. For example, during the Reformation, Tudor monarchs in England frequently used the clergy to preach sermons that conveyed political messages.[8] More recently the British, French, and Germans have all tried to use pan-Islamic ideology for their own ends. A perfect example of this was the British diplomatic pressure on the Ottoman caliph that produced a proclamation declaring the British empire as Dar al-Islam in 1857 – a declaration that fatally undermined the ideological underpinning of the rebellious Muslim nawabs in India, which in turn directly contributed to the demise of the Indian Mutiny or First War of Independence.[9]

So, while religion has been a useful tool for individual European governments in the past in achieving their foreign policy aims and extending their internal control, the history of the struggle for dominance between church and temporal authorities has produced a deep-seated desire to keep the church out of the public square, for fear of allowing its influence to spread once again. It is into this ongoing conflict that Islam has dropped, with its blend of faith and state, adding a new dimension to a struggle that had appeared all but won by a secular government which is now having to engage with the issue afresh, both in relation to security specifically and the impact of immigration more broadly.

State replacing church

It is therefore clear that, because of the long struggle European rulers have had with the church over control of all aspects of life, a deeply ingrained fear of the church returning to that control has set in among officials and politicians across Europe. Yet, ironically, even in these deliberately non-religious governing philosophies, attempts to throw out religion have actually resulted in quasi-religious governments.

In his 2006 book *Earthly Powers* the historian Michael Burleigh traces attempts by mankind throughout history to create systems of government which are not "religious" in and of themselves, but which resulted in quasi-religious states that mined religion for its linguistic conceptions.[10] Burleigh quoted from the German historian and philosopher Eric Voegelin who used the term "political religion" to describe the development of communism, fascism, and national socialism. Voegelin tried to show how the language and symbolism of religion, even when it's rejected, is still co-opted for use by non-religious regimes. Burleigh argues that the collectives which replaced the church in Western society included race, state, and nation, and that they adopted the language which used to be used for the church:

> These new collectives of race, state and nation also perpetuated the symbolic language which linked in this world with the next world, including such terms as hierarchy and order, the community as "church", a collective sense of "chosenness", mission and purpose, the struggle between good and evil transmitted into secular terms, and so forth.[11]

It was not that Christianity was rejected and religion disappeared; it was actually that Christianity was replaced by a different "religiousness".

So, even as our modern "secular societies" have sought to reject "religion", we could say that they don't seem to have found a better chord for binding us together than the repackaged version of the one they were so keen to reject in the first place.

Nevertheless, whatever might be said about the co-opting of religious language, the basic fact of "religion" being seen as a threat to the authority of the "secular" state has continued, reborn in this century as a result of the alarm felt by governments across Europe at the spectre of religious radicalization, whether that be identified in Islamic terrorism or in an emboldened and publicly active Christian evangelicalism. In public discourse this has manifested itself in two ways: first, that the church is seen as an institution of control; and secondly, that all religions are viewed as essentially the same and, by definition, just as dangerous as each other. This narrative has come to the fore in relation to the advent of Islam in the West, where those in government have seen it become an emblematic element of this recast church-state struggle. We'll get to the dangers of that perception at the end of the book, but for now let's turn to answering the accusation of negative church influence: the basis of the claim that the death of Christianity would be beneficial for society.

Is the church controlling?

Even though a good deal of the church's political power was lost hundreds of years ago, much of the debate about the church's "control" is really focused around the influence of its doctrines on those who follow it, or feel bound to it. In our current age this is often (though by no means exclusively) expressed in relation to female emancipation.

One of the most vocal and able antagonists to public religion, in this and other regards, is the journalist and social commentator Polly Toynbee of *The Guardian* newspaper, whom I therefore quote at some length in the hope that this will give us a sense of the types of criticism or accusation being levelled at Christianity (and other religions).

> *Women's bodies are the common battleground, symbols of all religions' authority and identity. Cover them up with veil or burqa, keep them from the altar, shave their heads, give them ritual baths, church them, make them walk a step behind, subject them to men's authority, keep priests celibately free of women, unclean and unworthy. Eve is the cause of all temptation in Abrahamic faiths. Only by suppressing women can priests and imams hold down the power of sex, the flesh and the devil.*[12]

Here she is writing on sexuality and the sex drive:

> *Trying to deny the primal life force has led to centuries of persecution, suffering, secrecy and breathtaking hypocrisy. Wherever male cultural leaders hold absolute and unscrutinised power, women and children will be abused. In western secular life this has at last been recognised: in schools, prisons, care homes and within families, wherever the powerless are unseen and unheard, horrors will happen without checks and transparency. Abusers gravitate towards*

> *closed organisations, and absolute power*
> *turns people into abusers. But the Vatican*
> *still talks of a few bad apples requiring*
> *internal discipline, the pope refusing to hand*
> *rapists over to secular law.[13]*

This concern over the freedoms of women and the denial of natural sexuality feeds a wider discourse about the role of religion when it is connected with power:

> *Wherever religion controls politics it drives*
> *out tolerance and basic human rights. The*
> *history of Christianity has been the perfect*
> *exemplar, a force for repression whenever*
> *it holds any political sway. It only turns*
> *peace-loving when it is powerless.[14]*

This is certainly something that some people feel keenly. For example, a report from a 2014 secularist conference in America described the emotions of some of its female attendees:

> *Women talked about "coming out," being*
> *open with their families, leaving "the*
> *closet" at a conference here this month.*
> *But the topic was not sexuality. Instead,*
> *the women, attending the third Women in*
> *Secularism conference, were talking about*
> *being atheists. Some grew up Catholic,*

some Jewish, some Protestant – but nearly
all described journeys of acknowledging
atheism first to themselves, then to loved
ones. Going public was a last, often
painful, step. Anyone leaving a close-knit
belief-based community risks parental
disappointment, rejection by friends and
relatives, and charges of self-loathing.[15]

This is another theme that those opposed to religion in public life are desperate to establish: the idea that religion is something forced on to a general public who widely resent it. Polly Toynbee again:

Religion imposed on the rest of us is
profoundly resented by the great majority.
Take schools, where a third are under
religious control… Selection makes them
popular, yet even so a majority want them
abolished.

Or on assisted dying:

Lord Falconer's bill on assisted dying comes
to the Lords in June, but it's almost certain
to be killed off again by the bishops and the
religious lobby, despite overwhelming public
support over many years.[16]

Religion is the bad boy, preventing what everyone else apparently wants. Furthermore, its sinister power seems to be growing over a number of areas; of particular concern for opponents of faith is education, because of its influence over the shaping of successive generations:

> *The power of religion in education is growing, not shrinking, even faster than under Tony Blair. The Al-Madinah free school in Derby that collapsed as "dysfunctional" a year after opening demanded all women staff wear headscarves, and segregated boys and girls in class and canteen – girls at the back. Michael Gove has sanctioned six new Islamic free schools. How could he not, when he has rapidly increased both the number and proportion of faith schools, to over a third, most of them Christian? British Social Attitudes research finds 73% of respondents opposed to all religious state schools; yet once in place, faith schools are never dismantled by local mergers or closures.*[17]

Reading these quotes we could be forgiven for thinking that the church is in the process of a subtle take-over – one the vast majority of people would certainly be opposed to if they were only made aware. So we need to test the truth of these alarmist claims. After all, if they are true, then they are a serious cause for concern. But if false, they should not be allowed to go unchallenged.

Learning new numbers

So are the advocates for the ending of faith schools, such as the British Humanist Association (BHA), carrying out a struggle on behalf of a silent majority?

In a poll on faith schools in the UK, taken by YouGov on behalf of the "Westminster Faith Debates" series in June 2013, over 4,000 people were asked whether the government should fund faith schools across different faiths. One particular sector that received a positive response was Church of England faith schools (42% said government should fund places, against 38% who thought they shouldn't). Furthermore, most of those polled (49% agreeing with the statement, 38% disagreeing, and 13% "don't know") said that it was acceptable for faith schools to give preference to "children from families who profess or practise the religion with whom the school is affiliated".[18]

Both of these statistics fly in the face of the apparently "overwhelming support" that the BHA says it has for the ending of "faith schools". But the statistic from the YouGov poll which most undermines their case comes in the final question: "Some people have suggested that all faith schools should admit a proportion of students who follow a different religion or no religion at all." The question then gave a number of options which ranged from "all faith schools should have to adopt this policy" to "it is better for faith schools to admit pupils only of the same faith". The poll found that 30% (the majority in this case) felt it was up to the school to decide whether to adopt that policy, as compared to 26% who felt there should be no faith schools at all, and a further 23% who agreed with the statement at the beginning of the question. So at the very best the evidence of this poll suggests that there was some support for the ending of faith schools altogether, but actually it was in no way the ringing endorsement of the BHA's campaign that had been suggested.

The wave of popular support that secularists apparently ride on is weaker than they would want to admit. Most importantly, this data reminds us that secularists might not be defending the views of the majority at all; they are merely seeking to advance their own narrow agenda under the guise of defending others.

Of course, the BHA are not the only ones who have ever sought to sway people by boosting their imagined supporter base and providing a one-sided view of the work of the church in the UK.

Revisualizing the past

History, it is often said, is written by the victor. We only have to look at the case of the unfairly maligned Richard III to see the truth of that statement – a man whose reputation was made by his arch-enemies, his Tudor successors, not least the peerless William Shakespeare.

With that in mind, I want to argue that the same maxim can be applied to our view of the church in the Middle Ages. This is important because, in order to be able to argue that the death of the church is actually going to be a benefit to society, you have to believe the propaganda that tells us that the church was a force for bad when it did have a strong influence in public life.

If we want evidence of that narrative, we need only cast a quick glance at the plethora of portrayals of churchmen in TV dramas and films. For example, the TV adaptation of Ken Follett's *Pillars of the Earth*, mentioned in Chapter 2, contained one churchman who was conniving and greedy along with another who was fanatical and ambitious (even if he was also helpful in the community). Of course, there's no doubt that such people existed in the church at that time, as they have done all through the ages, but the portrayal was one-sided and did not reflect that of the original book at all, for the author had spent a lot of time detailing the care the monks were giving through the hospital and in the community as the cathedral was built – little of which was shown in the series.

This is just one example, but we have also had innumerable books, plays, and films about the Tudor or Reformation period. Many of them have focused around the corruption and power struggles within the church (*The Borgias*) and at court (*The Tudors, The Other Boleyn Girl, Wolf Hall*, as well as books by Phillippa Gregory and C. J. Sansom). Or else they have sought to show the emergence of modernist thinking in the teeth of deathly opposition from the church (*1492*). Now, there is no denying that these stories are based on fact, but the problem is that there is no drama which seeks to show the other side of the church: the deep, grass-roots pastoral care in the lives of communities up and down the country – something that continues to be its hallmark today, as we shall consider shortly.

Of course, we must recognize that drama has to hold our attention, and "everyday" stories by themselves would fail in this regard. Furthermore, it should be acknowledged that there have been attempts (especially in recent years) to explore the life of the church at more of a community or grass-roots level through humour (*Rev, The Vicar of Dibley*) or in documentary (*A Country Parish*). But these modern windows into parish life do not disrupt the narrative of the past which the "new establishment" peddles: the narrative which says that when the church had any power it was a force for repression and ignorance.

The comedies I just mentioned all take place in the present, in a time when power has been removed from the church and it is safely confined to "doing good" and the occasional pricking of our consciences. But what if the narrative of the past could be clarified with a more rounded picture of what the church was really like when it both held power and did its grass-roots work? Would it answer the accusation against the church that it was a force for repression, or would it underline the truth of it?

Our knowledge of the past is surprisingly patchy, even for the more recent past such as the Middle Ages. Studies of "church history" in the UK are many, and they vary from the more academic to the popular. Many of these histories look at one aspect of church life, particularly the organization and power relationships in the parish – as seen in Katherine French's *The People of the Parish: Community Life in a Late Medieval English Diocese*, published in 2001; or C. N. L. Brooke's *Churches and Churchmen in Mediaeval Europe* (1999). Others have looked at the development of Christian doctrine and thought in the medieval period: James Sheppard's *Christendom at the Crossroads: The Medieval Era* (2005) is a good example, or Jonathan Hill's general history of the development of Christian thought, which includes the medieval period in his narrative.[19] But there have been very few books (academic or otherwise) that have sought to capture the everyday work of the local priest or monk in his local community. Because of this focus upon power, structure, and doctrine, and lack of description of what we might term the "welfare" work of the church, we could be forgiven for thinking that all the church was obsessed with was creating and maintaining as much control of the country as possible.

Our view of the church in the past has been conditioned by the subject-focus of historians and the fact that power struggles make for far more interesting stories than those of everyday community interaction.

Thankfully, some of these gaps are starting to be filled in. In 2010 the history department at the University of York produced a detailed, comprehensive study of parish church life from the earliest years of Christianity's time in Britain through to the late twentieth century.[20] This remarkable collection of text and visuals was published in the form of a DVD Rom rather than simply being put into a book.

The collection, which includes contributions from over 200 academics, paints a more rounded picture of the church – one that is not simply about the struggles among the elites of society, which are there as well and which we described earlier, but also about the community care and succour that was offered to the poor and destitute in society. So, while it does present a vivid and comprehensive picture of the workings and machinations of church hierarchy (the part frequently explored in television and cinema), it also depicts the day-to-day welfare, health, and educational work that was being done year after year by priests, monks, and friars in conjunction with local philanthropists.

This University of York publication therefore shows us that the church was right at the heart of life in the community through its parish system. Local priests, nuns, friars, and monks tended the sick, cared for the destitute, and provided sanctuary for those afflicted by war. The church was intimately involved in the life of the communities around it, although this is not to say that everyone attended services, as we'll see in Chapter 7.

Jean Manco's website "Building History" talks about the fact that medieval hospitals actually did far more than modern NHS hospitals do:

They were a charity in concrete form…
[For] while the modern hospital provides
medical care, many medieval hospitals were
founded simply for the poor. They provided
a home for those too handicapped or elderly
to work – people who might otherwise have
to beg in the streets if their families could
not care for them. Other hospitals took in
the stranger. They were hostels for pilgrims
and other wayfarers.[21]

It is a bold claim and is evidenced in *A History of Pastoral Care* which gives detailed accounts of the pastoral activity of the church throughout the Middle Ages.[22] The book directly links Christian doctrine with this activity as it took place all over Christian Europe throughout the medieval period.

So the church was caring for society in accordance with the teachings of Christ in relation to illness, welfare and providing sanctuary for the poor and destitute. Sad, then, and unjust, that nearly all we get to see of the medieval church represented to us is the conniving and the repression on the part of the power-hungry who saw the church as little more than a vehicle to serve their own ambitions.

This was vividly portrayed in the film *1492* where, in a very powerful scene at the beginning of the film, we see two "heretics" being burnt at the stake, watched over by a pitiless cleric. Now, we don't want to downplay in any way the fact that such terrible punishments were meted out –

even once was once too often. But the impression we are given is that such punishments were commonly used to repress a population that the church neither cared about nor helped in any way. As we have seen, that representation is highly subjective.

Indeed it's not just wrong or misleading, it's dangerous; for this lopsided picture almost inevitably leads to the view that the "new establishment" would like us to take: that we are better off without the church. For, in order to want to see the end of Christianity, we would need to be convinced that it is ultimately a force for bad in the West – just as Polly Toynbee and the BHA clearly believe.

So this desire to see an end to the church in the UK has its roots in the struggles between state and church. A struggle which is fought in the modern era as a propaganda campaign, which casts the triumph of the "secular" state as a win for society at large over a dangerous and malignant controlling figure.

As we have seen, this is not reflective of the true picture historically and, as we shall see in the following chapter, it is not true today.

CHAPTER 5

Service and Power

We have already looked at how unbalanced the new establishment's portrayal of the past is, and we'll spend Chapter 7 talking about the narrative of "progress" that is peddled along with it. But first we need to look at the church's work in the present. Otherwise there is a danger we might think that the care we evidenced in the last chapter for the Middle Ages has somehow disappeared in the present. It's important to see that, even though the circumstances have changed, the church has continued to do this grass roots work: there is continuity of service, whether the church as an institution has held power or not. The church remains the force for good that it has always been through the ages.

Church schools

If we take the arena of education for example, we see that one quarter of primary schools and one-sixteenth of all secondary schools in England are Church of England schools. This means that about a million children are being educated in Church of England schools. In a recent survey for the Church of England, which sought to discover what people thought of their schools, 72% of respondents felt that Church of England schools helped young people grow into responsible members of society, and 80% felt that they promote good behaviour and positive attitudes.[1]

Voluntary service

This service to society in education is also seen in voluntary service. Churchgoers of all denominations contribute 23.2 million hours of voluntary service to communities every month, which includes providing activities for children outside of church worship (such as toddler groups and youth clubs) for 407,000 children under sixteen and a further 32,000 between the ages of seventeen and twenty-five. That number includes just under half of all toddler and pre-school children (up to age three), for that is how many attend groups on church premises, the vast majority of which are church run. This activity, which uses the services of over 115,000 volunteers, is a considerable portion of those 23.2 million voluntary hours.

Charitable giving

It is not just time that churchgoers give. Church of England congregations alone give £51 million per year to a vast array of charities. Some of this undoubtedly goes into the food banks which have risen so swiftly in hard economic times. A report written by Hannah Lambie of Coventry University highlighted the fact that the large majority of food banks arose out of a faith (Christian) perspective.[2] This is underlined by a fact that the Church Urban Fund revealed in a 2010 survey: over 82% of parishes have been asked for help by people in their communities and have provided "informal support". This support will include such things as:

- 40% of parishes who have been asked to help with those experiencing problems of isolation and loneliness;

- 69% who provide assistance with school work;

- 54% who offer care for the elderly;

- 35% who offer formal or informal assistance with debt problems and homelessness;

- 42% who offer assistance with domestic abuse;

- 38% who offer assistance with alcohol abuse;

- 58% who help with issues of family breakdown or "poor parenting";

- 68% who offer assistance with self-esteem issues and provide hope.[3]

This is all the more impressive as the vast majority of the statistics are those which cover the Church of England alone.

All these numbers highlight the extent to which the church (of whatever denomination) still plays a valued and active social role in communities all over the UK.

Furthermore, they serve as a counter-balance to the very one-sided story of church involvement in British life that we are in the process of analysing, and highlight the fact that the evidence points to a church that is just as engaged today in the communities of Britain as those in the past.

The church and freedom to choose

So, what of this question of the church's desire for power and control? As has already been acknowledged, it is an accusation that has some foundation in history. But the point about the new establishment's accusation is that church repression is part and parcel of Christianity. So is there such a thing as a "Christian model for political power" which advocates the acquisition of power and its maintenance through repression – one that might even be traced back to the founder himself?

In Mark 1:15 Jesus is recorded as saying, "The time has come... The kingdom of God has come near. Repent and believe the good news."

Does that mean that Jesus and his disciples accepted a political headship? And when people became Christians, did that "mark territory" at the same time as producing faith?

Well, not according to the words later attributed to Jesus in the Gospel of John (18:36). Jesus is being questioned by the Roman governor Pilate following his arrest, and he says,

My kingdom is not of this world. If it were,
my servants would fight to prevent my
arrest by the Jewish leaders. But now my
kingdom is from another place.

It seems Jesus' teaching on authority was focused around a call to people to accept the teaching that he was bringing and the free gift of salvation that he was offering. If someone accepted that gift then they voluntarily offered to put themselves under the rule of God – but not a rule that had political teeth on earth.

Of course, this is a teaching with enormous political implications, even as it deliberately steps away from attempting to take political power. One of the reasons that the Romans later persecuted the Christians was that they could not get their heads around the fact that when Christians called Jesus their "Lord" it was not a challenge to the headship of the emperor. The Roman emperor demanded absolute loyalty of his subjects and so, when someone else was being styled "Lord", that was a problem.

As it happens, Jesus had been very specific about calling on his followers to be grateful to their political masters, even though to say so made him deeply unpopular with those Jews who were desperate to see Roman authority deposed. In Mark 12:13–17 Jesus responded to a question about loyalty to political authority with this answer:

Whose image is this? And whose
inscription? ... Give back to Caesar what is
Caesar's and to God what is God's.

Fundamentally, Christians owe loyalty to the state – even an oppressive one such as the Roman empire – because they enjoy the benefits, such as protection from outside aggression. So Jesus' teaching is not about trying to create some earthly power base, but rather putting oneself voluntarily under the authority of God first. In practical terms, of course, this frequently brings about tensions, especially when the state demands more than it should, such as when the Roman emperors demanded sole loyalty – arguably, soul loyalty. But tension mounts also when what might be termed questions of conscience (today's "freedom of religion" issues) bring the believer into conflict with state law. Abortion, Sunday trading, and the wide range of issues around education and sexual relations, are high-profile examples of what are frequently battle grounds between faith and the law. But while these are causes of conflict, they are not tantamount to creating a "Christian" political state.

That said, life is not so simple. There is no denying that there are some Christians who would dearly love to swap the current pluralist legal settlement that exists in the West for a resurrection of the ancient laws of the Bible as found in Exodus and Leviticus. Furthermore, they would want to see Christians as government heads. Notable among these are the theonomists (also called dominionists or reconstructionists). However, their desire to see the moral and legal codes of the Old Testament reapplied in our modern era would not be supported by the majority of Christians, even though the origins of the movement can be found in what might be described as traditional or conservative American Christian circles.[4]

Theonomism can trace its roots to R. J. Rushdoony's book *The Institutes of Biblical Law,* published in 1973. In this eight-hundred-page work Rushdoony expounded upon the Ten Commandments and their application in the current age. Since Rushdoony's death in 2001 his daughter's husband, Gary North, has taken up the shaping and honing of the theonomist concepts. These include some of the traditional foundational beliefs such as the divinity of Jesus and the doctrine of the Trinity; but he adds the necessity of re-instituting the system of law governing family, civic life, and government that can be found in Exodus and Deuteronomy.

Such views (on the re-introduction of the Mosaic law) are impossible to justify theologically, yet this has not stopped Rushdoony and his acolytes from spending considerable time and energy in trying to do exactly that.

Christian views on a Christian perspective of government are far better represented in Britain in the widely varying policies of known Christian Prime Ministers, such as David Cameron, Tony Blair, and Margaret Thatcher. None of them (as far as we are aware) has had any thought of trying to achieve what the theonomists want, and all three had very differing views on what government should be about. In Britain, this variation among Prime Ministers would be characteristic of Christians in general, who do not align themselves with any one political party.

In America the situation is slightly different, as the

religious conviction of the President is a significant political issue. Both President Obama and President Bush before him have called themselves Christians; in fact it would be hard to find an American president who did not profess Christian leanings at the very least. Nevertheless, even in the United States where faith and questions of morality play central roles in electioneering, there has been no attempt to impose a federalized law based on the opening books of the Bible.

Why is that? After all, the church has had times when it has sought to vie for political authority. Surely with a Christian in power the temptation to make Britain or the US a "Christian country" again – in terms not just of culture but of law – must be almost overwhelming?

Of course, we can't guess what goes through the minds of the President or Prime Minister, but it would be good to believe that, whatever their personal desires might be in terms of wanting people to believe in the grace of Jesus, politically they prefer the present settlement because they would affirm that in a representative democracy (as opposed to a totalitarian regime) we have as close a representation as we could hope to find of what Jesus meant by the words "my kingdom is not of this world". Such a stance encourages the state to be no more than it really is: it positions rulers as office-holders, accountable to all for their decisions; and it enables all the elements that make up society – such as family, religion, culture, and government – to be simply constituent parts of a whole, rather than having government trying to control everything.

The freedom to choose loyalty is enshrined in the story

of the garden of Eden found at the beginning of the Bible. Man and Woman were placed in a garden that contained a tree which would give them knowledge (and to some extent powers) not originally granted by God. We might reasonably ask why God would deliberately choose to put temptation in their way and then punish Adam and Eve when they succumbed. I think the reason is very simple: he wanted Man and Woman to choose to be in relationship with him; he wanted their love, not just their obedience. If God had wanted them simply to be under his authority, he could have achieved this by removing any opportunity to make choices. By enabling choice he gave them the relationship option.

This basic principle underlines the nature of that much desired quality, freedom – the ability to choose; whether it be what you're going to wear today, or which government you're going to vote for. This is where the theonomists get it so wrong, because they advocate the imposition of ideals rather than the free choice that Jesus taught.

So, coming back to the question of whether the repression and power that have been a part of church history are "Christian", in line with the teaching of its founder, the biblical evidence points to an emphatic "no".

Perhaps this all makes sense of the remarks made by Mahatma Gandhi when a reporter asked him about Christianity.

"What do you make of the founder?"

"I'm very impressed."

"And what do you make of his followers?"

"I'm very unimpressed."

Now, Gandhi was fighting for freedom from an empire which had nothing more than a veneer of Christianity, and his remarks would have been governed in part by that. Had he seen the kind of welfare and community work we looked at earlier, it would be nice to think he might have made a different response. Nevertheless, the response of the Mahatma would likely be echoed by many.

However, the bottom line for us is that the belief that the country would be better off without the church is based upon a one-sided view of history and a lack of knowledge of Christian teaching.

Who says the church is controlling?

So, from a "new establishment" perspective, is the struggle against religion really the struggle against controlling institutions in the church, or is it against the practice of individual believers?

Given what we have seen above, the answer should be "some elements of the hierarchy", but in reality the answer appears to be "both".

In 2009 the British think-tank "Intelligence2" hosted a public debate (attended by 2,500 people) at the Central Methodist Hall, Westminster. The motion was: "The Catholic Church is a force for good in the world."[5] For the motion were the British politician Ann Widdecombe and the Archbishop of Abuja, Nigeria. Against were actor and broadcaster Stephen Fry along with author and journalist

Christopher Hitchens. A poll of all the attendees was taken before and after the debate, and they showed that Fry and Hitchens had clearly made a very persuasive case, because over the course of the debate those against the motion increased by more than 770 – an increase which meant that two-thirds of attendees left the hall having decided that the Catholic Church was not a force for good. So, what was it that Hitchens and Fry said that persuaded so many people to change their minds?

Hitchens went first and used the words of the papal apology issued by Pope John Paul II in 2000 concerning church abuses as the door through which he could list all the sins that had been committed over the last millennium and a half. It was a long list and included such well-aired entries as the Inquisition, the refusal to accept Galileo's observations, the forced conversion of South American natives, and the Vatican's silence over the Nazis' "final solution". It also included failings surrounding the child abuse committed by priests across multiple parts of the Western world, the atrocities in Rwanda (described as "the most Catholic country in Africa"), and the spread of AIDS due to the Catholic Church's teaching on the use of condoms. Hitchens finished with a more personal reference to Stephen Fry's homosexuality, pointing out that under Catholic teaching Fry's nature would prevent him from being a member of the Catholic Church. In closing he made a jibe at the papal doctrine of infallibility.

Fry was generally more conciliatory in his address, and it was by far the more subtle attack, for instead of generating a list of historical or current misdemeanours (although they were still inserted as asides) he kept his argument personal. In essence he was asking for sympathy at being characterized as "evil" (Fry's word) for his homosexuality, while at the same time arguing that the only reason the Catholic Church held such sway over people was because those who followed its doctrines were largely kept in ignorance and poverty.

His arguments followed a train of thought that we've encountered already – the church as a controlling institution. (The second of his arguments – the equating of religion with ignorance – is dealt with in Chapter 8.) The use of this line of argument by Hitchens and Fry should wake us up to the realization that this narrative of a controlling, repressive, and ultimately merciless church has been allowed to take root in the popular consciousness, not simply in some dusty academic backwater. It is an energetic, high-profile narrative, and clearly highly persuasive. We won't go over the responses that were given by those defending the motion, some of which were useful and some rather obscure, but I hope that, if nothing else, we have been warned: whether it be in the world of the political "new establishment" or of the "new atheists", a one-sided narrative about a "controlling" church has managed to embed itself deep into the public psyche.

For all these reasons we should not be surprised that there are many who have cause to fear the re-emergence of the church in public life. It is a fear that has become entrenched in the absence of counter-argument from Christians.

As a result of this deep-seated fear of the church's return

to a supposed place of public control, Christians have not been allowed to voice their opinions without being shouted down. This has been something of a shock for those who believe that the public square is neutral towards Christianity. The articles we have looked at, accusing religion of being a force for ill, along with numerous others in publications such as *The New York Times* and the *Washington Post*, demonstrate that the public space is not neutral at all. If we wanted verification of that statement, we need only look at the extensive coverage given to the Catholic abuse claims, which are never balanced by stories of the daily acts of charity and grace performed by Christians in all parts of the community. So the "new atheists" have been assisted in their efforts to hasten the church's demise by the officials and politicians who have inherited the struggle for control of the public space and are keen to ensure that the church is never able to re-enter that sphere.

CHAPTER 6

Religion and Violence

This chapter will take on another aspect of the narrative embedded among some in the "new establishment" – that religion has been the principal cause of strife throughout history, and so in encouraging "the death of religion" they are actually helping humanity. Clearly Islamic terrorism is a current spotlight for this narrative, but frequent referencing of the medieval Crusades and the Reformation wars that so damaged Europe in the sixteenth and seventeenth centuries have become well-worn hooks on which to hang this argument.

Indeed, it is not just the manifestation of violence in the name of religion that's the issue; religion is also seen as a societal divider which stands in the way of achieving the properly unified societies everyone wants.

I will argue instead that these "evidences" are actually examples of the struggle for power and control which are a natural part of human nature; and that, rather than pointing at religion, we could put man-made philosophies such as communism also as a prime motivator for conquest and power. So rather than cherry-picking some useful historical events, if we want to have an informed debate about Christianity as a cause of violence, we need to argue about the principles enshrined in the philosophy or faiths themselves.

Old struggle, new century

In his book about the rise of the so-called "new atheists" Alister McGrath observes that 9/11 was a seminal moment for those, like Richard Dawkins, who had been arguing for years that religion was a dangerous influence in the world.[1] In the wake of the attacks, as McGrath shows, the phrase "Islamic terrorism" was adjusted to "religious terrorism" and then simply "religion". Dawkins more than inferred that violence was the natural outworking of religion in his article shortly after 9/11:

> *To fill a world with religion or religions*
> *of the Abrahamic kind, is like littering*
> *the streets with loaded guns. Do not be*
> *surprised if they are used.*[2]

Years later Polly Toynbee expressed the same sentiment in her *Guardian* column: "Wherever the institutions of religion wield real power, they prove a force for cruelty and hypocrisy."[3]

This same argument is made in Chapter 2 of the international bestseller by Christopher Hitchens, *God Is*

Not Great (2007) with great self-righteous abandon. The chapter opens with a quote from the Roman Lucretius, "To such heights of evil are men driven by religion", which is presumably there to show that there have always been those that have felt this way. Lucretius lived at a time when there certainly were some incredibly cruel things done in the name of religion: we only have to think of the practice of child sacrifice to Moloch in the ancient Near East (as recorded in the Bible), or the pagan human sacrifices practised by the druids in the vast forests of northern Europe, or the oceans of human blood spilt on the Aztec altars of South America. But it should be remembered that there are few cultures that have had as strong a blood-lust as Lucretius' own Roman one, where it was purported in the name of "entertainment", rather than religion.

The core of what Hitchens is arguing in the early part of his chapter is a scatter-gun blast of accusations which include the charges of hypocrisy and violence, based largely on either Hitchens' own experience (the hypocrisy) or a quick side-swipe at the culpability of the Church of England "for the Crusades, for the persecution of Catholics, Jews and Dissenters, and the combat against science and reason" (the violence).[4]

Hitchens is clear that religion must by its very nature interfere in the lives of other people. It cannot help itself, as he goes on to say: "It may speak about the bliss of the next world, but it wants power in this one." An observation which he explains with the remark: "This is only to be expected. It is after all wholly man-made." The rest of the chapter becomes essentially a catalogue of all the terrible things he has witnessed around the world, all of which had been done in the name of religion. Hitchens was careful to include all religions, and made sure his examples were from many differing parts of the world (all of which, strangely, began with the letter "B", such as Belfast, Belgrade, and Beirut). It is certainly a sorry catalogue, although it might have been more balanced if Hitchens had included the repression and violence associated with other places such as Beijing. But of course that would have been antithetical to the point he was making.

I will just point out two inter-connected things that we'll return to a little later: first, Hitchens tries to paint all religions as exactly the same. It is an argument that would be laughed out of town if it were made about political philosophies, so why is it reasonable here? Secondly, Hitchens makes no attempt to find out whether the killings that he was describing were justified on the basis of the doctrines of the faith or not. All of the faiths he was talking about have teachings or scriptures in the public domain. It is therefore entirely possible to find out whether, in each of the cases he names, the people perpetrating the violence could legitimately claim to be doing so on behalf of their faith or not. And, if not, then it would not be unreasonable to say that those actions Hitchens cites as evidence for religiously inspired violence could be more correctly labelled as human opportunism in which religion becomes an excuse.

A similar line to Hitchens was taken by the author Sam

Harris who achieved notoriety with his book *The End of Faith* in 2004. The core of Harris's argument was that "religion" was the reason for the 9/11 attacks. Of course there was an acknowledgment that radical Islam was the trigger for 9/11 itself, but Harris echoed Dawkins' words in laying the wider blame for the attacks on the inherently violent and irrational nature of all religion. In Harris's eyes religion is inherently dangerous because it stirs up emotions so strong that it must eventually cause such terrible events as 9/11.[5] The thrust of Harris's position was to set himself up in opposition to religion as the mere outworking of superstition and lack of reason. For him, all religion was coming from the same place, and that place had no room for reason.

In the paperback edition of his book, produced a year after the original, Harris took the opportunity to counter some initial criticisms of his argument. He was at pains to point out that his work was not to "convert" people to "blind atheism" in some parallel way to their previous blind faith. No, the nobility of his cause lay in the fact that he was encouraging people to think, to use their minds, and so come to the inevitable conclusion that religion must be wrong.[6]

The Dawkins, Hitchens, and Harris narrative seems to have struck a chord. An article for the *Guardian* newspaper by Julian Glover in 2006 brought home the evidence of the impact of Dawkins and others, for it contained a poll in which 82% of respondents said that they saw "religion as a cause of division and tension between people".[7] The same thing was seen on Channel 4's *Gogglebox* on 7 October 2014 when Judith, the mother of the Malone family in Manchester,

voiced the views of many: "I think John Lennon was right...
Religion causes war. Well, not religion, but the way people
interpret it. If there was no religion, there would be no war."
Dom Parker added, "Abolish all churches – do away with it."

So the Harris, Hitchens, and Dawkins narrative seems to
have hit home. As Karen Armstrong said in the introduction
to her book *Fields of Blood*, "In the West the idea that religion
is inherently violent is now taken for granted and seems self-
evident."[8]

This argument needs to be refuted. Such one-eyed
perspectives should not be allowed the oxygen they need
to misdirect and confuse. For, quite apart from the rather
insulting intimation that anybody who believes in a religion
must have laid aside their critical faculties, Harris's argument
flies in the face of the very reason he claims to serve.

Killing for Jesus?

We won't look at Islam, Judaism, or the Brahmanic faiths in
relation to this debate about whether religion is the cause
of violence, partly because this is a book about Christianity
specifically and also because it is really for people from
within those faiths to answer such criticisms for themselves,
appealing to their own scriptures and traditions.

So, in order to check whether Christianity as a faith can
be culpable for acts of violence, rather than people cloaking
their own blood-lust, greed, or ambition in the mantle of
faith, we need to analyse its teachings.

Beginning at the beginning, therefore, there seems to be little room for misinterpretation in the teachings of Jesus. He was very clear that violence in his name could not be justified, right up to the point of his arrest when he rebuked his disciple for taking out a sword to defend Jesus (Matthew 26:52). Similarly in Luke 6:27–31 Jesus makes his views on violence crystal clear:

> *But to you who are listening I say: love your*
> *enemies, do good to those who hate you,*
> *bless those who curse you, pray for those*
> *who ill-treat you. If someone slaps you on*
> *one cheek, turn to them the other also. If*
> *someone takes your coat, do not withhold*
> *your shirt from them. Give to everyone who*
> *asks you, and if anyone takes what belongs*
> *to you, do not demand it back. Do to others*
> *as you would have them do to you.*

There are many who would see this as a kind of "door-mat charter": an invitation for Christians to accept bullying and repression without seeking justice, or without standing up for what they believe. But leaving that aside, the teaching leaves no room for violence on behalf of Jesus. Jesus was not opposed to all violence at any time (although he didn't take any life), for John 2:13–16 records that the same Jesus got so angry with those ripping off the people who had come to make sacrifices at the Temple in Jerusalem that

> *he made a whip out of cords, and drove*
> *all from the temple courts, both sheep and*
> *cattle; he scattered the coins of the money-*
> *changers and overturned their tables. To*
> *those who sold doves he said, "Get these out*
> *of here! Stop turning my Father's house into*
> *a market!"*

Furthermore, in Luke 22:36 he exhorted his disciples: "But now if you have a purse, take it, and also a bag; and if you don't have a sword, sell your cloak and buy one."

Nor did Jesus rebuke the job of the soldier when he came into contact with them in his ministry (such as Matthew 8:5–10).

But perhaps the words of Jesus which do appear to leave the door open to violence are those found in Matthew 10:34: "Do not suppose that I have come to bring peace to the earth. I did not come to bring peace, but a sword."

On the face of it, these words seem to be a clear contradiction of the teachings he gave elsewhere. And yet, if we read further, in the very next verse Jesus' use of the word "sword" becomes clear, for he is not talking about violence at all; rather, he is acknowledging that his teachings have the potential to divide families and whole communities. This is not because his teachings deliberately seek to split up and destroy. Jesus is simply acknowledging that some will accept his teaching and others will not – and that acceptance or rejection will have consequences.

This is a theme which is repeated later in the New

Testament, where Christians are exhorted to prepare themselves for the spiritual battle in which they are involved by putting on "the armour of God" which includes in its list of equipment "the sword of the Spirit, which is the word of God" (Ephesians 6:17).

Evidence that Jesus' words bring division are not hard to find. Just ask those from non-Christian backgrounds who have chosen to follow Jesus. Their choice has often (though not always) meant expulsion from the family or community in which they grew up.[9] So, while Jesus' teachings do not exhort violence, that does not mean that they will not cause division and tension.

Some Christians have seen in Jesus' teachings a call to outright pacifism in all circumstances. Others, however, also see in Jesus' words a justification for violence when used in defence.[10] The teachings of the Apostle Paul enlarge on this in Romans 12:18: "If it is possible, as far as it depends on you, live at peace with everyone."

However, as that injunction allows, there may be times when violence to defend the innocent is not just allowable, but a duty, as Paul makes clear in Roman 13:1–4:

> *Let everyone be subject to the governing*
> *authorities, for there is no authority except*
> *that which God has established. The*
> *authorities that exist have been established*
> *by God. Consequently, whoever rebels*
> *against the authority is rebelling against*
> *what God has instituted, and those who do*

*so will bring judgment on themselves. For
rulers hold no terror for those who do
right, but for those who do wrong. Do
you want to be free from fear of the one
in authority? Then do what is right and
you will be commended. For the one in
authority is God's servant for your good.
But if you do wrong, be afraid, for rulers
do not bear the sword for no reason. They
are God's servants, agents of wrath to bring
punishment on the wrongdoer.*

But let's be clear – this is not war to extend the "power of Christianity" (we've looked at Jesus' statement that his kingdom is not of this world) or to force people to convert. This is about the legitimate need of police and military forces, entrusted by the government to keep law and order and defend its people. So we might see the participation of the Allied armies of the Second World War as an obvious outworking of that teaching.

It would be hard to deny that this teaching would rule out the Crusades in terms of legitimate uses of violence on behalf of Christianity. For all that we might want to excuse the Crusades as "of their time", the fact of them remains. Nor is it a case of just one isolated incident: there were numerous Crusades throughout the Middle Ages, whether to Jerusalem, in Russia, Spain, or those waged against "heretics" such as the Cathars of southern France.[11]

So, on the surface at least – whether we say Jesus taught non-violence or limited, defensive violence – there is more than enough historical evidence to show that some Christians saw no obstacle in Jesus' teachings to wars in the name of Christianity. And, as wrong as we would now argue this violence was, we have to acknowledge its existence. However, in doing so we need to also make clear that there can be no justification for the charge that Christianity – in other words, the teaching of Christ – is the cause of war. The fact that this has happened in the name of Christianity does not make it the fault of the doctrines of Christianity, but it does mean that the church needs to acknowledge its errors, both past and present.

That's something Pope John Paul II did during his pontificate (which as we saw in the previous chapter was used by Christopher Hitchens in the Intelligence2 debate). Edward Stourton's biography records that Pope John Paul made numerous apologies, not just to Muslims for the Crusades but also to Jews for the pogroms and for the silence of many Catholics during the Holocaust. He also apologized to Africans on behalf of those Catholics involved in the slave trade, and for those burned at the stake up to and including the Reformation period.[12]

Is religion a cause of war?

So Christianity cannot be said to be a cause of war. But is it *part* of the cause? Might "religion" as a whole have been the major cause of war in history, and does that therefore implicate Christianity, seeing it is the religion with the largest number of adherents in the world?

I think the answer would still be "no".

Even if we were to accept the notion that any action committed in the name of the religion must be blamed upon that religion, whether the religion teaches such things or not, then other factors surely rank higher as a cause of violence: the lust for power (including securing economic resources), dynastic rivalry, and systematic conquest, to name but three.

Take, for example, the conquests of Alexander the Great, Julius Caesar, Napoleon Bonaparte; and then add in the destruction of the Anglo-French Wars in the Middle Ages and early Renaissance, as well as the dynastic wars across Italy before it was unified. And this is mainly Europe – we haven't got to the rest of the world.[13] We would have blood spilt in gallons. Furthermore, if we include the vast destruction of the Mongol invasions, two world wars, and the dynastic struggles that raged over India, Asia, and Africa, we would have a good case for saying that wars in the name of religion could not possibly match the destruction caused by non-religious wars.

By way of putting numbers to the names we could take the data from scaruffi.com, which lists all the wars of the twentieth and twenty-first centuries with their approximate casualties. Piero Scaruffi, the website's founder, gives the total number of deaths in war over this century (plus a bit) as 160 million. Some of the numbers he cites, such as the

Ottoman slaughter of the Armenians and Stalin's purges, should perhaps not be included as "casualties of war"; however, putting aside this quibble, and also removing violence that has a clear religious element such as the Hindu-Muslim slaughter around Indian independence in 1947, the number arrived at for non-religious deaths is still well over 130 million. That compares with (at the most) 2 million for religiously related violence. This figure also includes events such as the Intifada, India-Pakistan clashes, Northern Ireland, and the Balkans.[14]

Now this is not to be blasé. Any death and destruction is awful, whatever the reason, but it serves to highlight the ludicrous nature of the "new atheist" claim. The difference between the two figures is not just significant, it's a gaping chasm. So we must reject the argument that religion is the major cause of violence in the world.

And with that goes the notion that religion needs to be removed because (as Judith Malone put it) "if there was no religion, there would be no war". For, as we have seen, clearly that is nonsense.

So, having exploded the myth that religion is a major source of violence, we need to move on and turn our attention to another facet of the argument for the benefits of church demise: that the church is the enemy of progress.

CHAPTER 7

Who is the Enemy of Progress?

Having looked at the arguments that violence and control are inherent to Christianity, we come to what is probably the main reason why Christian growth is not being reported: the view that the survival of religion is anathema to the Marxist narrative of human "progress".

This is a notion that we all seemed to have swallowed whole. It is a narrative in which religion becomes defunct as technology and science permit the light of knowledge to flood into the dark ignorance of religion and superstition. Marx argued that history shows that human progress has been made when the fear and superstition which exercised control over populations is replaced by more sophisticated and rational thinking. Thinking which did not simply lead to development in the structure of societies, but which also benefited humanity through technological advances.

In this chapter we shall trace the pervasion of this narrative in various areas of our political, cultural, and social life, even finding it in the church, before we go on to see how we might wean ourselves off this alluring narrative. To do so we'll make use of evidence reminding us that atheism is nothing new, while conversely there are plenty of people in senior scientific positions who have a strong faith. We shall see that people in centuries gone by were not universally superstitious, or uninquisitive, but many questioned the world around them. In other words, the scientific mindset is not a phenomenon which had to wait for Christianity to be pushed to the margins of public life.

The majority of this chapter will be concerned with unpacking the theories and construction of what has become known as the "secularization thesis". This is a construct of the social sciences based around the observation of and research into the Christian retreat from the public space, along with the mapping of shifting religious allegiances. The final part of the chapter will be given over to directly answering the accusation that Christianity is a barrier to human progress and the bettering of humanity – known in the terms of the Universal Declaration of Human Rights as "human flourishing".

The appliance of science

The concept of "secularization" didn't really begin as the belief that we now associate with the word – a belief in the inevitable destruction of the church. Rather, it began quite innocuously with the realization by Max Weber (and others) that, when we look back into history we see that supernatural explanations for events or phenomena were gradually put to one side in favour of rational ones, often involving calculation. This happened with increasing regularity to the point where it became the norm. So, for example, instead of looking to God's hatred of human sin for the cause of a particular flood, scientists and geographers explored the effects of different climatic and ecological dynamics on water-tables.

In 1967, the same year as *Sgt Pepper's Lonely Hearts Club Band* was released, the American sociologist Larry Shiner encapsulated the core of the implications of secularization when he wrote that it heralded "the decline of religion" in which "previously accepted symbols, doctrines and institutions lose their prestige and influence. The culmination of secularisation would be a religionless society".[1]

When Weber initially noted the shift from "superstitious" to "rational" explanation he did not argue that the church had been its enemy – he simply noted the phenomenon. Others in his field were not so open-minded.

The famous psychoanalyst Sigmund Freud directly connected what we might term a "religious mindset" with a lack of scientific enquiry. He argued in his earliest book about religion, *Obsessive Actions and Religious Practices* (1907), that religion and neurosis are similar products of the human mind. Neurosis manifests as compulsive behaviour, and as such is "an individual religiosity"; while religion could be characterized as a "universal obsessional neurosis".[2] He saw in the observances of religion a way of trying to cope with the chaos and seeming randomness of life around us. It was a concept he developed later in *The Future of an Illusion* (1927) where he referred to religion as "an illusion" which he considered, almost admiringly, "perhaps the most important item in the psychical inventory of a civilisation". For to Freud religion provided a comfort against "the crushingly superior force of nature", and he concluded that all religious beliefs were "illusions and insusceptible of proof".[3]

According to Freud's account, as fear changed to questioning and observation, "mystery" became a thing to be conquered rather than revel in and adore. It was this process of "disenchantment and rationalization" to which Weber gave the term "secularization", although it appeared only rarely in his writings.[4] Swatos and Christiano summarized Weber's thinking with these words:

> *Weber's claim is that appeals to divine authority have lost credibility relative to the past as providing a sure knowledge for social action, and that practical economic considerations (as contrasted to a heavy bank account) have come to play an increasing role when coming to measure the worth of knowledge.*[5]

So, this shifting ground of "secularization" had two elements. The first simply involved the observation that religion was no longer the go-to place for explanations of how the world around us worked. The second, however, concerned itself with blaming religion for seeking to prevent humankind from finding those rational explanations. One element of secularization was therefore about research and observation; the other was about blame and accusation.

For those interested in observation alone, scholars in the discipline of the "sociology of religion" have developed and defended (under increasing criticism) the arguments about the shifts away from religious explanation made initially by Weber. As part of this developing theory of "secularization", the narrative of religion's inevitable demise has become an uncontested "truth" which has, until very recently, been cemented in the writings of Bryan Wilson, Steve Bruce, and Ernest Gellner. These academics have implicitly assumed the inevitability of religion's demise. All they have differed on are the causes of that demise.

Bryan Wilson has been keen to argue that religious systems (all of them) have experienced a decline in influence so severe that it will be impossible to reverse. He argued that they have been replaced by individualism: a kind of consumerism in spirituality to match the consumerist spirit in other aspects of life.

Ernest Gellner has seen it slightly differently, even though he was broadly in agreement with the Weber hypothesis. He argued that scientific advances have enabled us to live lives of relative luxury which, in turn, have given us the space to explore the metaphysical. In many respects he is reiterating the famous concept of Marx, that "religion is the opium of the people". In this perception religion becomes an add-on, which can serve a useful function in binding societies together, but is not the foundational basis for life that it would have us believe.

From this point of view, satisfying our physical needs takes precedence over every other consideration.

Also in this view religious opinion has increasingly become *an* opinion rather than *the* authority upon which to base actions. This was summarized very neatly by the Aberdeen University scholar Steve Bruce in his review of David Goodhew's book, *Church Growth in Britain*, where he highlighted the fact that, although sociologists of religion have given different weight to various factors, all of them broadly agree that the trend has been towards the marginalization of religion.[6]

Furthermore, Weber and others saw that this process of secularization wasn't simply intellectual but also political: this was the period in which the state began to acquire more of the roles that had previously been done by the church – such as welfare, health, and education. So the mental separation went hand in hand with a desire to make sure that the church was kept more to the margins, away from the centre of society. This was a little different in the US where the constitutional separation of state and faith had not formally occurred – a dynamic which ensured that the threat of Christianity "interfering" in the civil public life of the nation would not be viewed the same way as in Europe.

This way of thinking is perhaps best encapsulated by Karl Lowith's argument that progress can be defined as the "secularisation of Hebrew and Christian beliefs".[7] Lowith's views were broadly in line with those of Nietzsche, of whom he was a devoted pupil, in so far as Lowith's fundamental desire was to see Judeo-Christianity (which he equated with ignorance) replaced by a return to Greek enquiry.

Charles Taylor captures the essence of these ideas in his famous book *The Secular Age* in which he offers three slightly differing views of secularization: first, religion is something that is in retreat in the current age; or alternatively, secularization itself might be a belief which is "regressing"; thirdly, also alternatively, secularization is under scrutiny at the present time.[8] The fact that he rejects the notion of secularization is useful to bear in mind, and we have looked at some of the evidence which enabled Taylor to argue instead that "our age is very far from settling into a comfortable unbelief".[9]

But all in all, perhaps it is the words of Daniel Chirot that sum up most succinctly the narrative that the ideology of "progress" brings us. In his *Religion and Progress* paper he looks towards a bright, religion-free tomorrow.

> *The future is always unpredictable, but it is good to remember two historical facts. The West's progress was dependent on freeing itself from religious dogma. Yet, the gains made by abandoning any inflexible and repressive set of imposed ideological values are always reversible because in troubled times many turn back to reassuring verities from the past.[10]*

So Chirot and Lowith's argument makes a neat segue into the counter-argument, because they capture the essence of so much – not just the arguments of commentators such as Max Weber and Grace Davie, but also those of the active proponents who desire to see an end to religion such as Lowith, Marx, Freud and, in more recent times, Dawkins, Hitchens, and Harris.

It is a potent narrative because it combines the discipline of scientific observation and enquiry with the energy of the zealot.

Remoulding the misshapen story

So let's pick apart the two facets of "secularization" that form the foundation upon which this theory is based: first, that religion was universally observed; and secondly, that a religious faith prevented intelligent engagement with scientific questions.

Back in 1851 the UK census asked a question about religion for the first time. The question was optional and, not surprisingly, the overwhelming majority who did complete the optional question (which was on a separate piece of paper) stated that they were Christian. However, as part of the same census process, a report was prepared which gave a snapshot of church attendance across the UK on Sunday 30 March 1851, the day of the general census. Their thorough research showed that approximately 8 million people attended church across all denominations – which at that time was 44% of the population.

This fact is fascinating. The visions of pre-war Britain we have is that church attendance was almost universal – not necessarily because Christianity was universally believed but because, socially, it was the right thing to do. We only have to pick up a book like *Pride and Prejudice* and see the characters attending church as a matter of course to see a depiction of this view.

Now, by modern standards the survey was a blunt instrument, in terms of finding the true religious beliefs of the population. For instance, how many regular churchgoers were bed-ridden or unable to attend? But it does give a glimpse of the possibility that there was no "blanket belief" across Victorian Britain before *The Origin of Species* came along and woke everyone up in 1857.

In fact there had been rumblings of discontent for nearly two centuries. The process of questioning and re-evaluating the doctrines of Christianity had been in motion since the development of humanism (in Italy and North Europe) in the fifteenth century. It was fed in no small part by Christians who wanted to understand the Bible for themselves, rather than being told what to think by the local priest or bishop, or the Pope himself. This critical thinking was daring and sometimes cost lives. But by the time of the 1851 census this critical enquiry had been augmented by the impact of nearly a century of the kind of first-base questioning that was the hallmark of the Enlightenment, where questions were employed that would be considered scientific, trying to nail down the evidence for the history which the Bible describes. So, it would not be unreasonable to argue that this critique of the doctrines and authenticity of Christianity – along with the later questioning of the existence of God – produced a raft of good reasons why people might not be attending church well before *The Origin of Species* was published.

But we can go back further than this – into the so-called "age of faith" – for Rodney Stark has shown that church attendance in the Middle Ages was by no means universal and might even have been less than today.[11] If proven, this is extraordinary. It's a view that turns our perception of the past on its head and forces us to think again about the kinds of stereotypes we have of our antecedents.

Critics of Stark's opinions have argued that we should not mistake faith for "religious culture" since the culture of faith infused everything – it was all around people, both those who believed and any who didn't.[12] The number of churches scattered over Britain and Europe testify that there may be truth in that criticism, but if we do accept that, it makes the evidence of *lack* of church attendance all the more remarkable. For in an age of high mortality (infant and other) through disease, war, and famine, people still apparently shunned the comfort of faith that was all around them. In modern parlance we could say they voted with their feet. Maybe they chose to seek comfort from each other rather than listen to the remote platitudes emanating from the pulpit of some richly attired bishop.

The sociologist John Sommerville attempted to answer Stark's evidence by pointing out that, whatever misdemeanours people were executed for, these were framed in religious terms – as a kind of heresy. In other words, and contrary to the evidence we've just looked at, people could only articulate their rebellion against the church by referencing other ("heretical") beliefs rather than ceasing to believe in God at all. For evidence he turned to a 1938 book by Lucien Febvre entitled *The Problem of Unbelief in the Sixteenth Century: The Religion of Rabelais* where he argued it was literally impossible not to believe during the period of Rabelais' lifetime – that to conceptualize the non-existence of God would have required a vocabulary that simply did not exist at that time. Sommerville captured the idea with a pithy phrase:

> *Modern faith might be measured by polls that asked people if they "believed in a God". The relevant question for medieval peasants would probably have been what they thought of God. To find out how (rather than whether) they were religious, one would ask whether they had made any vows recently, or said their prayers, or made their confession or pilgrimage, or "charmed" their fields or done any of the many things that showed one's religion.*[13]

Sommerville is arguing that it was inconceivable for the medieval peasant, landlord, soldier, or merchant to imagine a framework of existence which did not include God or the supernatural in some form.

As we have seen, Sommerville is not only wrong, but his

argument shows he is so wedded to the secularization theory that he cannot conceive of any kind of logic or personal free thinking outside of religion before the "modern era".

So, returning to the evidence presented by Stark: whatever the reasons behind medieval lack of attendance, the fact of it remains. If we wanted further proof, we should bear in mind that, such was the depth of the problem, a law was introduced in the throes of the Reformation to make church attendance and the learning of Bible passages compulsory.[14] Clearly this had a hugely political motive behind it – to ensure that the English population was thoroughly indoctrinated into the new theology that the Reformation had brought and which the Tudor monarchs had embraced. Nevertheless, the fact that the law had to be introduced in the first place is a testament to a lack of attendance that was rife.[15]

But what about the rest of the post-Reformation, pre-nineteenth-century period? On the surface, as I mentioned back in Chapter 4, the public space was in the process of being "cleared" of religion, and this gave the opportunity for different thinking. Here's Sommerville's commentary on Sir Isaac Newton's methodological approach to understanding space and time:

> *The fact that it was an Englishman who accomplished this may not be surprising given the fact that the religious geography of England was the first to be destroyed.*[16]

In other words, once religion had been removed, some real thinking could go on!

The problem is, Newton was a Christian, as indeed are many famous and well respected scientists and thinkers today. Does this simply mean he went to church as a matter of social convention? Well, not according to Charles Hummel, the author of *The Galileo Connection and Genesis: God's Creative Call*, who provides pretty convincing proof that not only was one of the world's best regarded scientists a Christian, but he spent more time on theology than he did on science.[17]

It seems, therefore, that science and religion were not in opposition as far as Newton was concerned.

But what of the post-1851 era – the era in which Darwin published *The Origin of Species* and Marx published *The Communist Manifesto*?

As I write, the centenary remembrances for the beginning of the First World War, the "war to end all wars", have been taking place. In the same year as that catastrophic, society-changing event, an academic paper by Eugene Lyman was published in the *Harvard Theological Review* which tried to wrestle with the vexed relationship that had been developing between those who were arguing for social progress and those who were encouraging adherence to what they believed religion taught about society.[18]

When Lyman was publishing his article, much of the debate about whether religion was a barrier to "progress" was not, as it is today, about whether Christian beliefs are true or not; it was concerned with whether the Bible could be seen as an enhancement to modern society or as an enemy of social change – the kind that Social Democrats wanted to see. Lyman pointed out that the argument that the Bible is an enemy to social "progress" is based upon the perception that all Christians are socially conservative:

> *Religion… is not by nature progressive, but*
> *conservative. It does not invent the new;*
> *it cherishes the old. It does not explore the*
> *unknown; it venerates the true, tried and*
> *well-known. Its work is not to originate, but*
> *to conserve, not to disturb the souls of men*
> *with infusions of energy, but to soothe them*
> *with the anointing of peace.*[19]

The charge is not without foundation, at least for the church historically: just ask Galileo Galilei, Girolamo Savonarola, or Christopher Columbus, all of whom, in their own ways, challenged the conventional wisdom at that time and found themselves in conflict with the church authorities. Reformers like Martin Luther and John Calvin were very concerned that the "right" (God-ordained) social order was maintained, even as they attacked the Roman Catholic Church for its teachings. Indeed, famously, Martin Luther refused to support a peasants' revolt against what they saw as the injustices of their lord, on the basis that they were upsetting what should have been the proper order of society.[20]

Leaving aside Luther's concern for the "good name" of Christ, there can be little doubt that the accusation of defending the status quo, rather than allowing progress, has some weight. But clearly the "charge" of "defending a social norm" is short-sighted if applied to Luther who was in the vanguard of completely shaking up the political structure of the day. Luther's supporters were drawn from all levels of society – from Frederick III, Elector of Saxony, to the peasants overburdened with church taxes. The idea that Christians such as Luther and Calvin were opposed to any kind of change in society is simply fallacious. What perhaps we could say, however, is that the Protestant Reformers were keen on correcting what they felt had gone wrong, rather than wanting to make changes simply for the sake of making changes.

We need to keep that in mind, even if we do associate Christianity with "social conservatism", for this concept of "rocking the boat without turning it over" is a consistent theme throughout Christian history. For, while it would be fair to say that Christians have been supporters of a fair amount of "tradition" in the UK, it needs to be acknowledged that this support is largely based on the fact that the law and ethics of the state have borne a close relationship with what has been described as "Judeo-Christian" morality. As that changes, it is also likely that what has been seen as a Christian defence of the status quo will shift and become much more of an advocacy for change. In that sense, modern-day Christians would be doing what Luther and Calvin would also have advocated.

Indeed the idea that Christianity is somehow wedded to the status quo or social conservatism could only really find any kind of fertile ground in places like Britain and the

US. Here Christianity has formed such deep roots that its teachings are part of the cultures in which we live. As soon as we step into places where Christianity is an "outsider" – such as the Middle East, China, or North Africa – we begin quickly to see how the message of Christ is a society-changer, not a defender of the status quo.

Comments like Lyman's simply show how deep the changes have been which Christianity has wrought in our culture, and how West-centric the entire debate on secularization is. Try telling the Roman emperors that the message of Christianity defended the status quo.

Let's remind ourselves how revolutionary the message of Jesus really is, and then highlight the number of Christians who have been at the forefront of social and scientific change. It may be that what we shall find undermines this "enemy of progress" narrative, instead of evidencing it.

Who's rocking the boat?

As we've touched on already, even going back to the earliest years of Christianity the Bible records the revolutionary nature of the Christian message in the ears of those who first heard it. The teachings of Jesus were a direct challenge to those who held both religious and political authority. After his lifetime, incidents such as the Apostle Paul being driven out of Ephesus after preaching and teaching (Acts 19:23–41), and the stoning of the first Christian martyr, Stephen, on the basis of his challenging words to the Jewish authorities (Acts 7:54–60), are typical of patterns that have been repeated down the centuries. These were words and lives that challenged the conventions of their day and continue to challenge the "norms" of our societies even now.

Sometimes, as we've seen, the church was a dominant political power as well as a religious one. At times its institutional authority was challenged by monarchs and rulers, some of whom may have had no faith at all. But the biggest furore arose from priests and monks, like Martin Luther, who challenged authority, even church authority, and stood up for what they believed in – even in the face of death. Thomas Becket and Thomas More, whether we agree with them or not, would be examples of this, as would (in a different context) William Wilberforce, whose tireless work to emancipate slaves is widely recognized.

But it is not just within the narrow confines of church doctrine and authority that Christians have sought to effect change. We can look at the world of mathematics and science for examples of pioneers and people who were happy to step out against prevailing wisdom as Christians. So Roger Bacon, the thirteenth-century philosopher, is credited with being one of the earliest proponents of scientific methodology – as was his colleague, William of Ockham, the Franciscan friar. Then there was William Turner, the so-called "father of English botany" who, in the Reformation period, was briefly Dean of Wells Cathedral before being thrown out for his non-conformity. In the world of chemistry, the seventeenth-century scientist Robert Boyle is recognized as a key figure in the development of that discipline. What is perhaps less well known is that he was also a theologian. And coming into the modern world, we owe a great debt to the work of the mathematician John Napier who, in addition to writing exegetical books on the Bible, was also the inventor of the logarithm.

All these are key people of science *and* people of faith who, even without the next name, would have dispelled the idea of science and Christianity being in opposition. And there are many more. But certainly Isaac Newton was, and still is, considered one of the greatest scientists in history, even though we know he spent much of his life researching and writing on the Bible.

We might go on. Michael Faraday helped to found electromagnetic theory – in addition to his church work. Mary Anning was a paleontologist responsible for the finds at Lyme Regis in the nineteenth century, and Henrietta Swann Leavitt was head of astronomy at Harvard. We also shouldn't omit Ernest Rutherford who has become known as the father of nuclear physics and was so honoured as a scientist that he was buried next to Isaac Newton in Westminster Abbey.

Today there are a number of eminent mathematicians and scientists at the top universities in the world who are also Christians: John Lennox and Andrew Briggs at Oxford would be two examples, along with the astronomer Jennifer Wiseman, chief project scientist for the Hubble telescope.

This sample (for that is all it is) exposes an important fallacy: that religion must give way to a rationalism represented by atheism.

It may be a neat connection: plausible and offering a narrative of history which flatters the human race (particularly in the West). But it doesn't fit with the facts. Though we might say that science has provided competition for faith, even augmented it, it has in no way replaced it. Moreover, it is clear that some of the greatest scientists were also men and women of faith. So this notion that science and faith cannot co-exist is not just wrong, it flies in the face of the evidence.

Let the facts speak

So looking at the facts, perhaps the notion that Christianity has opposed "progress" should be re-evaluated… maybe even thrown out altogether. Not least because the narrative of progress itself is highly questionable. Would it not be more factually accurate to talk in terms of a bumpy pattern of destruction and creation, followed by further destruction and creation? After all, the Romans in Britain were eventually followed by the Saxons and the Vikings – and with the best multiculturalist, values-free lenses that we could hope to see through, no one could argue that either of those two groups were a manifest improvement on what went before – especially in the area of health and sanitation.

This is not to say there haven't been measurable improvements in society, even if this is always dependent on your particular outlook. We need look no further than the comfort of our homes and the ease of travel and communication to see the new benefits that have softened life for so many of us. And it's not just in the realms of invention and health that our lives have changed for the better. Societies in Europe, the minority world, and the majority world beyond have all seen shifts in attitudes. The revulsion in many societies against slavery and public execution (especially as a form of entertainment) are proof positive of sharp shifts. Those places in the world that have representative governments are also manifestations of social and political shifts that have taken place.

Does all this signify "progress"? Of course it does. But that doesn't mean to say that these changes represent new thinking. Rather, they form a series of "tipping points" when attitudes that were valued as good for society were owned by more and more of the population, to the extent that fundamental, long-term change could occur.

The idea that Christianity as a religion has somehow opposed new thinking is simply wrong. Our relatively small sample of Christian scientists through the ages is proof enough of that, let alone social reformers like Lord Shaftesbury, William Wilberforce and Dr Thomas Barnardo.

So when the "new atheists" and other elements of the "new establishment" talk in terms of the church as the enemy of "progress" – in fact when we hear talk of the very notion of "progress" itself – let's pause for a moment and call to mind the assumptions and one-dimensional viewpoints that lie behind it.

CHAPTER 8

Re-embracing the Church

So far we have seen that the reports of the demise of Christianity in Britain are "exaggerated" to the point of outright error. We have also identified reasons why some might have a vested interest in perpetuating that error and seeking to encourage the demise of Christianity in the UK.

All very interesting, but where might this lead us, in practical terms? I see two areas where the outworking of these findings need to be considered.

First, given the life, energy, and national networks which the church retains, and given the country's current economic circumstances, it seems sensible to allow the church to re-engage in those areas of public service where it used to have a traditional role: welfare, education, and health. The burden on the state would be lessened and the church would be serving the country in a way that fits its ministry. The German arrangement in these areas makes for quite an interesting model around which to think of these issues, and we shall look at this later in the chapter.

However, if the church is to become involved in a more formal way, then legitimate concerns over the church attempting to achieve political power need to be allayed. Such fears are caused by concerns over past behaviour by both the Roman Catholic and Anglican Churches in the days when they held considerable institutional power. And in order to think about that, we need to discuss whether the time has come for the disestablishment of the Church of England.

My second practical outworking concerns religious literacy amongst policy-makers. The evidence for growth rather than decline highlights the fact that, as religious issues are not going to become redundant in the foreseeable future, there is an urgent need for a more nuanced understanding among policy-makers, so that some of the rather lazy suppositions around a "one size fits all" approach to religion can be replaced by something more realistic.

The benefit for the state

The church has always understood that part of its role is to serve the societies in which it is embedded. As we have already seen, during the Middle Ages this service included health, education, and welfare. But even in our modern era, when the church has been pushed out of public life, the church is still serving in education with a very high satisfaction rate. So, given that the church is not on the way out, and in the light of all that we have considered thus far, it seems only sensible to allow it to come back into other areas of its traditional role as well.

Of course, as soon as I make any such call, there will be almost apoplectic cries from among the "new establishment" – particularly the "new atheists" – who would, I'm sure, point out how "dangerous" such a move would be and talk darkly of the repression of "free thinking" which is apparently part and parcel of the church's psyche. Some of this I tackled in Chapter 4, and clearly no one would want a return to the kind of institutional power the church held in the Middle Ages. But we are potentially throwing the baby out with the bathwater here, for the same period that brought us burnings for heresy also brought us what we would now term "voluntary-sector-led" welfare and healthcare. This was the time when the church, along with grass-roots communities, took it upon themselves to look out for those in their parishes who were either sick or destitute. And today, in our "post-downturn" economic climate, the more welfare, healthcare, and education can be put into the hands of voluntary organizations, the greater the reductions to the nation's bills there will be.

In essence what I am proposing is a recasting of the "Big Society" concept that the Conservative Party made the centrepiece of their antidote to the country's economic woes. They realized that state control over all aspects of a nation's life comes at a cost – a cost which is unsustainable, hence the eye-watering deficits being run by almost every nation on earth.

But we don't have to turn the clock back four hundred years, culturally or politically, to find the benefits of having health, welfare, and education back in the voluntary or church sector, where no one needs to turn a profit in order to serve society. We only have to look across the water to Germany – which still has around 100,000 church-based charities who provide healthcare, education, and care for the elderly – to get some sense of how this might work for us in Britain.

In 2000 the academic Christine Barker wrote an article which explored the benefits and problems associated with the church-state settlement in modern Germany.[1] The meat of her analysis centred around whether the so-called *Kirchensteuer* (church tax) could still be justified in the changing society of modern Germany. This is a tax collected by the state and levied on all members of German churches (Catholic and Protestant) whose proceeds are then used to finance the church's administration of healthcare and welfare. The tax is collected on behalf of the church by the German government direct from pay-slips in the same way that other taxes are collected. It is then handed on to the Catholic Church and the Protestant churches.

In principle it is a system that works well. In practice, even though 67% of Germans belong to one of the churches, about 60% of them do not actually pay the tax because they are either unemployed, in prison, or on some form of welfare support – circumstances which automatically remove the burden of payment. So in reality, only 40% of the 67% are actually paying the tax. Clearly that means that there is less money to go around. It is also fair to say that there are numbers leaving the church. So the feasibility of confining the tax to those who are church members, rather than simply collecting the tax from all citizens and then giving the money to the church, must be questioned.[2] But, pragmatic issues aside, for our present purposes we will stick with discussing the principle rather than analysing whether the system is still workable. In fact I am not arguing that we transplant the German system to the UK anyway. What I am recommending is that we explore a version of that system.

So aside from issues of workability, there is a question of principle: is such a tax a fair way of funding the system?

Secular voices in Germany have argued that the tax is a form of coercion: that the tax is not the same as a gift, freely given. Clearly this criticism can be levelled at any tax. The right of the state to collect taxes for the provision of protection and services to its citizens has been debated over millennia, and to delve into that territory at this point would be a distraction. However, it is interesting to note that an article for the Centre for European Economic Research in 2009 argued that Christians in Germany were less likely to make charitable donations outside of the tax as, perhaps reasonably, they felt they were making their donations through the tax already.[3]

Others argue that, given that Germany seems to be increasingly defining itself in secular terms, the tax is now out of date. This criticism is not unlike the arguments being made by the BHA in the UK, so, without knowing how accurate the data on church decline is in Germany, it is impossible to debate the point.

There is, however, one criticism of the German system which would need to be addressed for a British context: some commentators in Germany feel that the *Kirchensteuer* creates too strong a relationship between church and state – not least that it robs the church of its political neutrality.

This is an important criticism and is part of the ongoing debate in Germany, so while the benefits of the German system seem plain, we need to deal with the legitimate concerns around the possible politicization of the church if some element of that system were to be implemented in Britain. For Britain this particularly revolves around the Church of England's "established" status, but before we get to that we ought to look briefly at how, in principle, the church in general might avoid the temptation to try to take political power on the back of its service to society.

I think there is an insurance policy against this happening, one element of which is the pluralism that has developed over the past four centuries. In other words, if the church attempted to convert its service to power, there would now be enough journalists, commentators, and politicians critical of the church to ensure that loud alarm bells would be rung. Moreover, the practice of "power" itself is now so much more diffuse in our global era than in the Middle Ages that the notion of any one institution taking such power is unrealistic.

That is not to say that the church could not – and does not – wield any influence at all; of course it does. The recent report by the National Intelligence Council *Global Trends 2030* highlighted that, with the reduction in the direct power of government institutions and the growing trend towards global outlooks (especially among the middle classes), it is likely that religious affiliations will have an increasing influence in the medium term.[4] So in calling a power coup unrealistic I realize I open myself to accusations of naivety, for yes, the church doubtless contains within its ranks many who could be tempted by the prospect of using service as an opportunity to acquire power. This could theoretically be a "road to hell paved with good intentions". However, it seems reasonable to suggest that there would be too many other influences, checks, and balances for the UK to become church-owned in any sense.

For this reason I can see only positive results in allowing the church to engage in the educational, welfare, and health elements of public life. Any government short of money and desperate to cut their structural deficits should look closely at this, as it could save them from having to hand over parts of their remit to companies whose primary motivation must be profit margin rather than service.

So, in essence, the church would be offering a service, not seeking to enrich itself. If we wanted an example from outside of Europe, or the West in general, we could look at India, where Christians are a tiny minority and structurally discriminated against, yet who nevertheless provide much of the health and education for peoples of all faiths and none. In fact, the figures are really quite astounding, prompting one Hindu to admit that, if the Christians left India, health and education provision in the country would probably collapse.[5]

The age-old conundrum

The issue of church-state relations in the UK has long been a hot potato, because inevitably it involves talking about the establishment or disestablishment of the Church of England, even though the Anglican Church is only one expression of church in the UK.

The UN Special Rapporteur on Religious Freedom, the former German university professor Heiner Bielefeldt, said that one of the most significant factors in restricting religious freedom was an official state religion, especially one that plays to narrow definitions of national identity.[6] We don't have to look far to discover that Bielefeldt's words have a lot of truth to them. We can look around the world at the moment and see numbers of examples, such as Greece, Russia, Israel, Pakistan, Saudi Arabia (in fact most of the MENA region), Myanmar, Malaysia, and Indonesia. Furthermore, if we look back into history, we can find even more examples from every inhabited continent. There is no state on earth, and no religion (including atheism), that has "clean hands" when it comes to this. And yet, if we look at the "established" nature of the Church of England, we should ask ourselves whether we can see its role as "repressive" in any way. I for one cannot.

Obviously, if the church-state relationship in the UK is not to be generally corrosive for society, we shall need to aim a lot higher than ensuring that the institution is not "repressive". But could the changes I'm suggesting be done without the Church of England being disestablished?

Well, the first thing to say is that we are not talking about just the Church of England being involved with the welfare, education, and healthcare. As we saw earlier, most of the growing elements of the church are in the "free church" and Pentecostal denominations (although the division is slightly artificial anyway as there are evangelicals and Pentecostals in the Church of England, Brethren, Methodist, Orthodox, and Catholic Churches). So, even if it was inclined to do so, there is little chance that the Church of England would be able to exercise control over these other bodies, as they are not under the authority of the Church of England. (Ironically, Muslims and Hindus are generally more in favour of the established status of the Church of England than most Christians.[7]) Indeed, the only route through which the Church of England could try to exercise oversight or control over other religious bodies is if legislation were introduced specifying that any government funding, or any charitable donations towards welfare, had to come through them.

Apart from the grants given by the government to any faith school (including Church of England ones) there has been one glimpse of this dynamic. In 2012 the Home Office gave the Church of England a grant of £5 million for its "Near Neighbours" programme, under the auspices of the "Prevent" strand of the CONTEST strategy.[8] Now, while this made some sense as a discreet project recognizing the important and long established role of the Church of England in relation to cohesion, it would be a far more dangerous precedent for the kind of scale that I am envisioning here.

So the money would need to be broadly channelled. But what about maintaining or scrapping the current status of the Church of England in this new model?

My feeling is that actually the established status could remain as it is, but that there might need to be some checks and balances to prevent possible future power-grabs. For while that isn't something that we could envisage happening for generations to come, one always has to take the long view and think about the unknown people who are going to continue the work into the future. Limits and frameworks are therefore vital.

For us to think about what these future refinements might be, we first need to understand what presently exists. So – for the benefit of those who do not understand the established status of the Church of England (which includes the majority of Christians) – let's try to get to the bottom of what "establishment" means in practice.

Perhaps it's best to go to that other pillar of the establishment, the BBC, for an objective definition. On its "Religions" web page the BBC cites three elements which give the Church of England its current status:

- the monarch is the Supreme Governor of the church;
- the church performs a number of official functions;
- church and state are linked.[9]

Some further detail is supplied for us by the Church of England's own website, which notes that the current constitutional place of the Church of England was created after the English Civil War and the period of the Republic in which the Puritans, led by Oliver Cromwell, actually persecuted the Church of England's clergy for siding with the Royalists. It wasn't until the Restoration under Charles II that the settlement we see today was established in 1689 through the Toleration Act. The act gave legal status to Protestants outside the Church of England and set out the privileges and responsibilities in the country for the Church of England. Later, over time, the legal status originally given to those Protestants has been extended to other Christians, other faiths, and those with no religious adherence at all.[10]

The two key pragmatic outworkings of "establishment" are that bishops are appointed by the Prime Minister and that some of its bishops sit in the House of Lords. Originally the House of Lords was a more or less equal divide between the Lords Spiritual (the archbishops and bishops) and the Lords Temporal (life peers and hereditary peers), but more recently the Lords has seen many more life peers added to its chambers, such that the Lords Spiritual are now a relatively small proportion of the total.[11]

Away from high politics, there are a number of other interesting historical rights and particularities that the Church of England enjoys. For example, the Church of England has a legislative body known as the General Synod which has the power to make laws, the most impactful of which also pass through Parliament for scrutiny.

But it's not all beneficial for the Church of England. For example, all building works and alterations have to have legal authority before they are carried out under the *Care of Churches and Ecclesiastical Jurisdiction Measure 1991*. At the grass-roots level, when a new vicar or priest-in-charge is appointed to a parish church, the bishop who appoints him or her not only commissions them at a special service, but gives them the "cure of souls" – a phrase that points to a level of responsibility for the spiritual health of all in the parish.

Those who argue for disestablishment (which includes a large number of Christians, particularly evangelicals) do so for a number of different reasons, many of which were captured in Adrian Hamilton's article which called for disestablishment as an antidote to falling numbers.[12] Of course, this book takes issue with Hamilton's characterization of the current state of affairs, but the argument he advances is one regularly heard in pews across the country: that even some of the senior clergy don't fully agree with its status because its official role encumbers it rather than assists it. It is an argument that was articulated again in 2012 very succinctly by Douglas Carswell, formerly of the Conservative Party and now an MP in the UK Independence Party. Writing in the *Evening Standard* he said:

> *I want the Church of England to break free*
> *from the State precisely because I want to*
> *see it prosper and thrive. Like the state-run*
> *industries in the 1970s, the Church of England*
> *has suffered from falling market share. It has*
> *expensive and costly overheads. It has failed to*
> *innovate, with sometimes complacent senior*
> *management. It has at times been in danger of*
> *losing touch with its customer base.*[13]

There is not much anyone would disagree with in this assessment of the Church of England's failings over generations (other than describing the Church of England in the same terms as a commercial company, perhaps). However, whether disestablishment would be an antidote or not is a different question.

But the broader principle is not an unreasonable one – history is littered with examples of churches which fell when the governments they were connected to fell. Just look at the French Revolution, or the experiences of the Catholic Church in Latin America at the end of the Spanish empire. However, there is no sense that the British system of government is likely to be revolutionized wholesale in the near future at least. So, in the absence of pressure to think fast and adapt to new circumstances, we can think this through soberly.

Apart from perceived mismanagement, is there anything else that should hasten the end of the Church of England's status?

We've already looked at one facet: the "narrative of decline" which we have shown to be wrong. Mind you, given that it is the evangelical and Pentecostal parts of the church that are growing, there may be a case to add Lords Spiritual from their number, as well as representatives from other faiths. But this could largely be accomplished from the "inside" by promoting the appropriate bishops. So there is no argument for wholesale change here.

Then what about the fact that, although the church has grown, so have atheism and deism (the belief that God is not personally involved with his world, or even a person at all)?

I don't think this is an argument for the disestablishment of the Church of England. The National Secular Society has had disestablishment as one of its "primary, long-term aims" on the following basis:

> *The existence of a legally-enshrined,*
> *national religion and established church*
> *privileges one part of the population, one*
> *institution and one set of beliefs. To remove*
> *all symbolic and institutional governmental*
> *ties with religion is the only way to ensure*
> *equal treatment not only to all religions but*
> *also to believers and non-believers.*[14]

Of course this is an articulation of the argument we have already met, which positions "new atheists" as the heroic defenders of the voiceless, while in actuality being a thinly veiled ploy to remove religion from the public square in the name of equality. As such, it is a clever strategy but, as we saw, they are calling for something that not even the members of the other faiths want.

For all the posturing about the ills of the Church of England historically, or the needs of equality currently, the guiding principle on disestablishment has to be one of the reasons behind church growth that we explored in Chapter 3. This revolves around the findings of Dr Roxane Gervais who concluded that spiritual wellbeing was an important facet of good mental health. If we migrate that principle to the "national health" of the country, then we must see that it is important for the "wellbeing of the country" that spiritual input should be included in the deliberations of its legislators.

Now, some will say that the same input could be guaranteed by ensuring that a number of Lords are maintained who come from a spiritual perspective. That may be true in theory. However, in practice it might be that a future Prime Minister or head of the Lords Appointments Committee may actually decide they don't want any Christians (or members of other faiths) to be in the House. In that case, as soon as the Church of England was disestablished, the presentations of Christian or spiritual perspectives into the vast array of policy areas that modern governments deal with could no longer be guaranteed. The input of spiritual perspectives into legislation would be subject to the whims of whoever happened to be in power, rather than constitutionally guaranteed as it is now.

At this point we should consider the example of the United States which has no established church. There can be no doubt that this "one nation under God" has the outworkings of Christian faith front and centre whenever elections are happening, and even in the normal course of political discourse. The importance of abortion as an electoral issue would be just one example of this. In the nineteenth century the French aristocrat and traveller Alexis de Tocqueville observed:

> *In the United States, the sovereign*
> *authority is religious... there is no country*

in the world where the Christian religion
retains a greater influence over the souls
of men than in America, and there can
be no greater proof of its utility and of its
conformity to human nature than that its
influence is powerfully felt over the most
enlightened and free nation of the earth.[15]

Now I would not wish to deny the fact that the US system has worked for Americans very well, certainly up to the present at least. But does this mean that doing away with the established church in Britain could also work?

I think the answer is no, and the main reason for that is the fact that America's cultural and constitutional psyche was shaped by two things: religious dissent, specifically the freedom to worship as they desired away from state control; and (fed by this) an ingrained suspicion of anything that smacked of central-government control of such freedom. The desire to hold on to faith was the founding desire of the United States in a way that it was not in the UK (or the rest of Europe). For that reason Christianity in America has an assured place (for the moment at least) in the public life or national wellbeing. The same cannot be said of Britain, even if we were to argue that the country's Protestant identity was valued for a time as a distinction against the control of the papacy. That identity has been eroded as a distinction over centuries as time has passed and the politics of the Reformation has made way for a new set of principles.

So the issue for the UK is how to maintain a spiritual input without the Americans' strong sense of need for the freedom of religion.

In those terms, I do not think that the Lords Spiritual can be bettered and so, rather than make change for change's sake, perhaps leaving the Church of England in its established status is the most sensible option.

All religions are not the same

My second point, to which I referred at the outset of this chapter, is so obvious that it shouldn't really need to be made, but clearly does in the light of the narratives we looked at in Chapter 4: We need greater religious literacy among all elements of the "new establishment" so that we can move away from treating all religions as one homogeneous mass. I believe we need to do this not only because it is disrespectful to faith groups but because it is a potentially harmful thing to do.

The wrong impression about any belief can become embedded in the psyche and provoke unreasonable criticisms or misconceptions of that particular faith. But, at a deeper level, treating all religions as the same will bring eternal consequence to the choices we make about faith. The religions of the world say such different things about the nature of God, the way to attain eternal life, or even whether there is eternal life, that for pure reasons of logic alone they cannot all be true. So a choice has to be made between them (or against them), and that choice will have everlasting consequences. Attempting to fudge the issue by trying to make out that all religions are the same only serves to confuse the most important question of our lives. Saying "what's right for you is not necessarily right for me" is all very well if you don't want a debate, but the possibility of eternal disappointment or suffering seems an awful price to pay for politeness.

We need to call to account the people of any faith who do things in its name, and to do that we need to have a reasonable level of understanding of each faith, rather than vaguely blaming "religion". We shall need to be doctrinal or scriptural about our criticisms: passages in the Old Testament in which Yahweh does not just permit violence but commands it need to be answered by Jews and Christians. The same is true for the Qur'an or Hadith in Islam, passages of which exhort the believer to violence in the name of the faith. They need to be critiqued and answered. The same of course applies to the non-Abrahamic faiths: for example, does the persecution of the Rohinga Muslims of Burma by Buddhist adherents have any basis in the teachings or doctrines of the faith? If so, it needs to be acknowledged and answered. And what about the caste system in India, which appears to enshrine inequality? Can that be specifically linked to Hindu theology? How should it be answered?

This would be an honest and rigorous approach to a vitally important issue, especially when we are seeking to answer the charge made by Dawkins, Harris, and others, that the very nature of "religion" makes "it" a wellspring for violence.

One final point about treating all religions as the same

when it comes to policymaking, particularly in the area of social cohesion: we need to be able to deal effectively with any doctrines that are antithetical to the kind of social harmony that governments are seeking. If all religions are treated as being the same, any blanket policy will miss its target.

Waking up to reality

So there are a variety of different issues that arise from seeing the picture as it really is, rather than fashioning it into something which suits a particular agenda or narrative.

There is no doubt that the church has been and may still be guilty of wrongdoing which should not be excused. But let us not paint a partial picture in the hope that it will lead to the death of a set of institutions which some find inconvenient. Instead, let's allow it to flourish as an even better example of what it has become: a servant of society in a position to help relieve the state of a financial burden.

CHAPTER 9

A Change of Perspective

My main desire in writing this book has been to do two things: to correct the mistaken impression given by the narrative of church decline in the UK; and to expose the underlying agenda that drives the lack of reporting of church growth and feeds the negativity towards the church. This has reached such epidemic levels that it has even penetrated into the psyche of the church itself. But has there been a deliberate conspiracy to mislead about church decline and the nature of that church?

Everyone loves a good conspiracy theory. Just think of the assassination of JFK or the persistent rumours that people didn't really land on the moon in 1969. Even theories that discuss ancient wrongs still get time and space: who really killed the princes in the Tower, and was it on the orders of Richard III or Henry VII? Was the young pharaoh Tutankhamun murdered? What ancient truths were lost in the fire at the great library in Alexandria?

In 2013 the American online polling company *publicpolicypolling.com* found that 37% of voters believed that global warming is a hoax; 6% believe Osama bin

Laden is still alive; 21% say a UFO crashed in Roswell in 1947 and the US government covered it up; 28% believe a secretive powerful elite with a globalist agenda is conspiring to rule the world one day through an authoritarian world government or New World Order; 28% believe Saddam Hussein was involved in the 9/11 attacks; 7% think the moon landing was faked; 13% of voters think Barack Obama is the anti-Christ; US voters are split 44%–45% on whether Bush intentionally misled the people about weapons of mass destruction in Iraq; 29% of voters believe aliens exist; 14% say the CIA was instrumental in creating the crack cocaine epidemic in America's inner cities in the 1980s; 9% think the government adds fluoride to the water supply for sinister reasons (not just dental health); 51% say a larger conspiracy was at work in the JFK assassination, with just 25% saying Oswald acted alone; 14% of voters believe in Bigfoot; 15% say the government or the media adds mind-controlling technology to TV broadcast signals (the so-called Tinfoil Hat crowd); 5% believe exhaust seen in the sky behind airplanes is actually chemicals sprayed by the government for sinister reasons; 5% believe that Paul McCartney died in 1966; 15% think the medical industry and the pharmaceutical industry "invent" new diseases to make money; 11% of voters believe the US government allowed 9/11 to happen, but 78% do not agree.

But if people like a good conspiracy theory, they love a good conspiracy that involves religion. Just ask Dan Brown or the raft of copy-cat authors who have made so much money from our taste for the mysterious and the forbidden. *The Da*

Vinci Code became the second-highest selling book of 2004 and the bestselling book of the decade (5.2 million copies).

Stories about the Templars have almost become an industry of their own, fuelled by Brown, Raymond Khoury, and a raft of others. Their books, along with histories and TV documentaries, have helped to keep this medieval order in the top twenty-five global "Google" searches consistently over the last decade.

Of course some of these theories arise from a natural curiosity: mankind's desire to know as much as we can about everything has brought us extraordinary scientific achievement. An instinct to find truth is as strong today as it was when Archimedes sat in his bath and had a brainwave. Other theories arise from a stubborn desire to find an alternative reality to the one that we have been peddled. Everyone from Copernicus and Galileo to Oliver Stone's obsessive interest in the assassination of JFK could come in that bracket. In fact, both of those examples are quite useful, because they illustrate the tendency to adopt a note of "scientific enquiry" to uncover good reasons to doubt the official versions of reality. But for others, it may simply be that the search for an alternative reality is the search for their own peace and a stubborn refusal to accept the truth.

In a world of twenty-four-hour media, a plethora of news websites, and a gaggle of spin-doctors "helping" us to interpret what we should be understanding about events around us, the search for "the real truth" as opposed to opinion has become even more important.

There is nothing quite so satisfying as to be able to expose a lie or a cover-up and be able to say, "I told you so." It is ennobling to keep searching and to one day find not only the truth but the vindication of your dogged determination to discover the truth.

When Bob Woodward and Carl Bernstein published their story about the Watergate break-ins, it had taken months of investigation against the backdrop of intimidation before they had been able to substantiate their claims. The subsequent furore and investigation brought down the Nixon government, spawned a bestselling book and box-office success – as well as giving us the suffix "gate" for a political scandal. If ever there was an example of someone not believing an official version and relentlessly pursuing the truth, the Watergate scandal must go down as one of the greatest validations of conspiracy theories in our modern era.

But in order to have a good conspiracy theory, we must also have a sense that what we have been told might not be true. Sometimes that process of uncovering the truth might not begin for years, even decades or centuries, because there is nothing available at the time to even begin to consider alternatives. Indeed, who knows what "facts" we "know" today will be laughed at in the future? Perhaps even some of the odd beliefs found in *publicpolicypolling.com* will be proven in years to come – however unlikely that is.

Returning to the present, however, this book has tried to unpick one "fact" that seems to have taken root and blossomed in the minds of the "new establishment" – those politicians, journalists, academics, and social commentators who form the foundation of what has also been termed the "metropolitan elite" in Britain. That supposed fact is the ongoing and inexorable decline of the church in Britain (and indeed the West in general).

For the peddling of that decline narrative to be considered a good conspiracy theory, rather than the correction of a simple mistake, there need to be foundations for an accusation of deliberate misleading and cover-up. And in order to prove that, there would need to be a reasonable explanation of why the error was more than a mistake.

I hope this book has provided both.

But one thing does need to be clarified before we finish: this book is not including all members of the "new establishment" in its accusation of mass misdirection. Some have simply followed the lead of others, and a few have even disagreed with the consensus. However, it is clear that a "truth" has been established which is nothing of the sort and that, moreover, there are a number of reasons to believe that contrary evidence has been either ignored or rubbished. This book has, I hope, set the record straight, as well as helping to clarify the agenda which underpins the deception.

Doubtless there will be many who argue with the figures I have presented and my interpretation of them. That is to be expected. But, if nothing else, I hope that this book has provided all of us with a profound realignment in perspective, ensuring that we look at the place of the church in Britain with both eyes open and not just one.

We began with sets of figures which, on the surface, painted a clear picture of church decline but which, on closer inspection and with the revelation of other figures, produced a quite different picture. Yet, when it comes to the narrative of church decline, that first set of figures has evolved into a "truth" that has been allowed to penetrate public discourse in the UK with little alternative argument being offered.

But do the facts match the perception? And is the removal of the church from the life of the nation really what most people desire? If it isn't, then why is it being pursued? And if it *is* widely desired, why might that be so?

In trying to get to the root of these questions the book has advanced two specific viewpoints.

First, I have argued that the obsession of some concerning the apparent control of the church, even in modern life, is founded on a long history of struggle between government and church over control in all aspects of public policy. It is a struggle which was won centuries back by non-religious authorities but which continues to deliver a psychological kick to those who fear the current re-emergence of religion.

Secondly, this fear is fuelled by an almost complete lack of balanced analysis about the work of the church – both in modern times and in history. My hope is that this has been at least partially corrected with the alternative sources and statistical evidence of the range and depth of the church's work in every part of every community in the country. But I recognize that it will probably take several reiterations before the one-sided story that has been ingrained for so long can be corrected.

I have not sought to defend the multiple inexcusable

actions committed by the church at any time, past or present. There can be no excuses for such actions, especially in an organization that was set up to reflect the grace-filled, sacrificial work of the God-man that Christians call "Saviour": Jesus the Christ. But when we are only presented with the bad stuff, we are bound to get a skewed view of the value of the church in our society.

What is more, when it comes to the political agenda which lies behind the desire to rid the country of the church, those who are not given the proper facts are in danger of agreeing to something which has only been partially presented. This can only increase the chances of throwing out the baby (the church's community work) with the bathwater (the institutional influence of the church in British society).

In fact we may now be able to discern that Dawkins, Harris, Hitchins, and others, far from being impartial and convinced by the reason they champion so vocally, are actually motivated by what was our final stopping point on our tour of their perspective: the narrative of progress. As we have seen, it is a narrative largely based on a Marxist-Leninist reading of history (itself open to question), and its conclusions have not so far produced governments that have allowed human beings to flourish – in stark contrast to the free societies which Christianity has helped to birth. It is a narrative which would keep us all religion-blind, so that we remain unable to discern the real impact of any of the world's religions which are summarily treated without the respect we afford the world's political ideologies.

I believe it is vital that these misconceptions and

inaccuracies be corrected, for two very practical reasons.

First, a misreading of the direction of travel among those who govern is likely to produce bad policy decisions. What do I mean by that? Governments attempt to steer and develop their countries by anticipating the direction of travel on a whole raft of aspects of daily life: for example, how will the internet change consumerism, politics, or ideology? Internet shopping is having a serious effect on our high streets. What, therefore, needs to be planned in terms of infrastructure, shifting labour-force skills, and population connectivity, in order that the nation is not left behind?

In the same way, the failure to understand and acknowledge that the inexorable move towards a secular, non-religious state in Britain seems very wide of the actual picture could potentially allow politicians to discount the concerns that Christians have concerning a range of medical and human rights issues. That is not to say that their views should be preferred, but rather, that we should guard against rushing towards legislation or policy on the assumption that the religious perspective is now less relevant. Of course not all religious people think the same way about the same thing, and within the faiths themselves there are a multitude of competing perspectives on almost any issue we could name. That said, however, there are commonalities (say, around the value of the family as an important unit for the welfare of society), and these would be common more or less across the board.

My second practical reason why these misconceptions should be corrected is this: rather than being fearful of the church and therefore trying to keep it at arm's length in society, it would be better to acknowledge the quiet, long-term, grass-roots work that the church has done for centuries over the length and breadth of the UK. This might then open the way to thinking seriously about taking full advantage of its service. At a time of desperate financial shortage, this would have a very clear benefit for the whole nation. We cannot let our fear of the past imprison us, or bankrupt us, either now or in the future.

Indeed, it is worthwhile noting that in our diverse society not even those of non-Christian faiths appear to have a problem with the "Christian" cultural foundation of Britain. The BBC reported the comment of Farooq Murad, Secretary General of the Muslim Council of Britain, that nobody could deny the UK remained a largely Christian country with "deep historical and structural links to Christianity". They also included the views of Anil Bhanot, Managing Director of the Hindu Council UK, who said that he was "very comfortable" with the UK being described as a Christian country. Indeed Bhanot added that "people can secularise those traditions but it doesn't take away from the fact that the country was based in Christian traditions".[1]

The idea that the church is far from dying out, and even showing signs of growth, is very unwelcome news to some. That is both a pity and a shame, and I hope this book has gone some way towards allaying the fears of those who see in the church an instrument of repression or even violence. There have always been good reasons for the church's active participation in society to be enjoyed and valued, once a proper picture of its activities is painted. So, whether or not my proposal of the German model of a reconstituted church role in society gets any traction, I hope all will see that an energetic, engaged church is something that can be enjoyed, not feared, in a society that claims to value the positive contributions made by all its citizens.

Notes

Dates are given for when online links were last accessed by the author; if a page has expired, you may wish to visit the website's home page and explore from there.

Introduction

1. For the purposes of this book we'll be using the definition of the "new establishment" which was articulated in Simon Kuper's article "The New British Establishment", *Financial Times*, 3 August 2012.

2. As reported in Joseph McCormick, "Nick Clegg celebrates 'equal marriage at last' despite 'dinosaur opposition' in the House of Lords", Pink News, 18 September 2013.

3. "Bishop says 'urgent action' needed to tackle church decline", www.bbc.co.uk/news, 21 September 2014.

4. The Office of National Statistics website has analysis of the statistics. See http://www.ons.gov.uk/ons/rel/census/2011-census/detailed-characteristics-for-local-authorities-in-england-and-wales/sty-religion.html (accessed 4 August 2014).

5. Oliver Hawkins, *Religion in Britain: Social Indicators*, Department for Communities and Local Government 2012. The same author wrote the updated report which features in the evidence of growth we shall examine later.

6. Todd Johnson, *Christianity in Global Context: Trends and Statistics*, Pew Research Center 2013, p. 1.

7. These surveys are reported on at the excellent "British Religion in Numbers" website http://www.brin.ac.uk/news/2014/roman-

catholic-and-other-statistics (posted 11 January 2014, accessed 15 September 2014).

8. Both survey results can be found at http://ukdataservice.ac.uk/get-data/key-data.aspx#/tab-uk-surveys (accessed 20 October 2014).

9. The data can be found at http://www.icmresearch.com/pdfs/2006_december_guardian_religion_poll.pdf (accessed 12 September 2014).

10. Jacinta Ashworth & Ian Farthing, *Churchgoing in the UK: A Research Report from Tearfund on Church Attendance in the UK*, Tearfund 2007.

11. David Barrett, "New figures show a sharp decline in Catholic baptism, ordinations and marriages", *Catholic Herald*, 17 May 2013.

12. As reported by http://www.christiantoday.com/article/researcher.anticipates.further.church.decline.in.2010s/25949.htm (posted 22 May 2010, accessed 21 September 2014).

13. Steve Doughty, "Just 800,000 worshippers attend a Church of England service on the average Sunday", *Mail online*, 22 March 2014. See www.dailymail.co.uk/news/article-2586596/Just-800-000-worshipers-attend-Church-England-service-average-Sunday.html#ixzz3CS7AV43s

Chapter 1

1. See David Voas and Laura Watt, *Numerical Change in Church Attendance: National, Local and Individual Factors* 2014. The report is available at http://www.churchgrowthresearch.org.uk/UserFiles/File/Reports/Report_Strands_1_2_rev2.pdf (accessed 13 March 2015).

2. *ibid.*

3. Oliver Hawkins, *Ethnicity and Religion Social Indicators Page*, London: Parliamentary Research Briefing, 8 September 2014.

4. John Micklethwait and Adrian Wooldridge, *God is Back: How the Global Rise of Faith is Changing the World*, London: Penguin 2012, pp. 134–39.

5. Micklethwait and Wooldridge, *God is Back,* p. 134.

6. Micklethwait and Wooldridge, *God is Back,* p. 135.

7. Matthew Bell, "Inside the Alpha Course – British Christianity's Biggest Success Story", *The Independent,* 31 March 2013.

8. According to http://uk-england.alpha.org/facts%20and%20 figures (accessed 4 September 2014).

9. See http://godandpoliticsuk.org/2013/05/08/the-church-of-englands-attendance-statistics-are-good-news-but-not-in-the-way-you-might-expect/ (posted 8 May 2013, accessed 12 September 2014).

10. John Pritchard (compiler), *Pocket Book of Prayers for Pilgrims,* London: Church House 2011.

11. Ian Bradley, *Pilgrimage: A Spiritual and Cultural Journey,* Oxford: Lion Hudson 2009.

12. Jane Alexander, "Easter 2009: Top Five Pilgrim Routes in Britain", *Daily Telegraph,* 9 April 2009.

13. http://www.arcworld.org/projects.asp?projectID=500 (posted June 2014, accessed 22 September 2014).

14. Peter Stanford, *The Extra Mile: A 21st Century Pilgrimage,* London, New York: Continuum 2010.

15. See http://www.christian-research.org/religious-trends/uk-church-overview/church-attendance-overview/ (no date, accessed 12 September 2014).

16. David Barrett, "New figures show a sharp decline in Catholic Baptism, ordinations and marriages", *Catholic Herald,* 17 May 2013.

17. The report is summarized at http://www.visabureau.com/uk/news/17-12-2009/study-into-uk-immigration-reveals-faith-of-migrant.aspx (accessed 14 August 2014).

18. Robert Booth, "Richer than St Paul's: church that attracts 8,000 congregation to a disused cinema", *The Guardian,* 11 April 2009.

19. See http://www.secularism.org.uk/news/2013/07/pentecostal
-churches-thriving-in-london-as-traditional-denominations-
decline (posted 31 July 2013, accessed 25 August 2014).

20. Andrew Rogers, *Being Built Together: A Story of New Black Majority Churches in the London Borough of Southwark*, London: University of Roehampton 2013, p. 19.

21. Holly Williams, "Hallelujah Southwark! The London borough is home to the highest concentration of African–Christian churches outside of the continent itself", *The Independent*, 25 May 2014.

22. Eric Kaufman, "Breeding for God", *Prospect* magazine, November 2006.

23. Eric Kaufman, "London: a rising island of religion in a secular sea?" http://www.demos.co.uk/blog/londonreligionsecularsea (no date, accessed 4 September 2014).

Chapter 2

1. As detailed in *Quadrant*, Spring 2014 at http://www.christian-research.org/uploads/quadrant/backcopies/Quad372014.pdf (accessed 3 September 2014).

2. Research and Statistics Department, Archbishop's Council, *Statistics for Mission 2012*, London: Church House 2014.

3. Available at http://www.methodistconference.org.uk/media/228157/conf-2014-37-statistics-for-mission.pdf (accessed 15 September 2014).

4. *Statistics for Mission*, p. 356.

5. Ian Randall "Baptist Growth in England" in Goodhew (ed.), *Church Growth*, p. 59.

6. *ibid*, p. 72.

7. See http://www.churchgrowth.org.uk/admin/userfiles/briefing_papers/Brethren_movement_Jan2013.pdf (posted January 2013, accessed 15 September 2014).

8. As found on the Scottish government's census portal http://www. scotland.gov.uk/Topics/People/Equality/Equalities/DataGrid/ Religion (accessed 1 October 2014).

9. Kenneth Roxburgh, "Growth Amidst Decline: Edinburgh's Churches and Scottish Culture" in Goodhew (ed.), *Church Growth*, p. 209.

10. *ibid*, pp. 216–17.

11. As found on the University of Ulster website http://cain.ulst. ac.uk/ni/religion.htm (accessed 1 October 2014).

12. Claire Mitchell, "Northern Irish Protestantism: Evangelical Vitality and Adaptation" in Goodhew (ed.), *Church Growth*, p. 237.

13. Emily Buchanan, "Church leader urges Iraqi Christians to quit country", *BBC News* at http://www.bbc.co.uk/news/uk-11705032 (posted 7 November 2010, accessed 20 October 2014).

14. Stephen Platten (ed.), *Dreaming Spires: Cathedrals in a New Age*, London: SPCK 2006.

15. Ken Follett, "Britain's soaring spires that became Ken Follett's Pillars Of The Earth", *Daily Mail*, 28 November 2010.

16. Opinion Research Business, *English Cathedral National Visitor Survey*, March 2010.

17. Grace Davie, *The Sociology of Religion*, London: Sage 2007, p. 146.

Chapter 3

1. As reported by Carol Midgely "Spirited away: why the end is nigh for religion", *The Times*, 4 November 2004.

2. *Globalization and Future Architectures: Mapping the Global Future 2020 Project*, Chatham House (Royal Institute of International Affairs) and National Intelligence Council 2005.

3. *Global Trends 2030*, National Intelligence Council 2012.

4. Anon, "UK is getting MORE religious, says Schama" at http://www.dailymail.co.uk/news/article-2666485/Historian-Simon-Schama-says-UK-religious-country.html#ixzz3D1MnLuK5 (24 June 2014, accessed 8 July 2014).

5. Just see the list of publications that cite the project on the University of Lancaster website http://www.lancaster.ac.uk/fss/projects/ieppp/kendal/outputs.htm (accessed 29 September 2014).

6. Michaela Robinson-Tate, "Yoga Outstripping Church Worship", *Westmorland Gazette*, 15 October 2004.

7. All the figures can be accessed at http://www.neighbourhood.statistics.gov.uk/HTMLDocs/dvc146/wrapper.html (accessed 22 September 2014).

8. Pew Research Center, "Millennials in Adulthood", 7 March 2014 available at http://www.pewsocialtrends.org/2014/03/07/millennials-in-adulthood (accessed 10 March 2015).

9. Roxane Gervais, "Religious Employees may be happier" at http://www.bps.org.uk/news/religious-employees-may-be-happier (posted 9 January 2014, accessed 21 September 2014).

10. Ed Stetzer, "The State of the Church in America: Hint: It's not dying" at http://www.christianitytoday.com/edstetzer/2013/october/state-of-american-church.html (1 October 2013, accessed 16 November 2014).

11. Steve McSwain, "Why nobody wants to go to church anymore" at http://www.huffingtonpost.com/steve-mcswain/why-nobody-wants-to-go-to_b_4086016.html (posted 14 October 2013, accessed 16 November 2014).

12. http://www.gallup.com/press/159062/god-alive.aspx (dated 4 December 2012, accessed 4 October 2014).

13. Micklethwait and Wooldridge, *God is Back*, p. 12.

14. Gary Langer, "Poll: Most Americans Say They're Christian" at

http://abcnews.go.com/US/story?id=90356 (dated 18 July 2014, accessed 4 October 2014).

15. http://edition.cnn.com/2009/LIVING/wayoflife/03/09/ us.religion.less.christian/index.html?iref=hpmostpop (posted 9 March 2009, accessed 4 October 2014).

16. Pew Research Center, "'Nones' on the Rise: One in Five Adults Have No Religious Affiliation", 9 October 2012.

17. Matt McGrath, "California blue whales bounce back to near historic numbers" at http://www.bbc.co.uk/news/science-environment-29069515 (posted 5 September 2014, accessed 23 September 2014).

Chapter 4

1. See Bruce Bueno de Mesquita, "Popes, Kings and Endogenous Institutions: The Concordat of Worms and the Origins of Sovereignty", *International Studies Review*, Vol. 2, No. 2., 2000, pp. 93–118.

2. This account is taken from Alexander Canduci, *Triumph and Tragedy: The Rise and Fall of Rome's Immortal Emperors,* St Leonards (NSW): Murdoch Books Pty Ltd 2010.

3. Carl Volz, *The Medieval Church: From the Dawn of the Middle Ages to the Eve of the Reformation,* Nashville (TN): Abingdon Press 1997.

4. David Abulafia, *Frederick II: A Medieval Emperor,* Oxford, New York: OUP 1988.

5. G. W. Bernard, *The King's Reformation: Henry VIII and the Remaking of the English Church,* New Haven CT: Yale University Press 2007, pp. 60–63.

6. The dynamics and historical progress of this trend are traced by Kaspar von Greyerz in his chapter "The Privatization of Piety" in *Religion and Culture in Early Modern Europe, 1500–1800,* Oxford, New York: OUP 2007.

7. Over the course of the debates concerning the banning of the Burqa in France, which have been ongoing since 1989, the 1905 law has been referenced a number of times. See Frank Tallett and Nicholas Atkin (eds.), *Religion, Society and Politics in France since 1789*, London: Hambledon Press 1991.

8. For example, see Stephen Chavura, *Tudor Protestant Political Thought, 1547–1603*, Leiden: Brill 2011, p. 86.

9. Clearly such tactics have not been confined to Europeans alone: the US funding of a "Holy War" against the Soviet invasion of Afghanistan in the 1980s is a well-documented example.

10. Michael Burleigh, *Earthly Powers: The Clash of Religion and Politics in Europe from the French Revolution to the Great War*, London: HarperCollins 2006.

11. Michael Burleigh, *Earthly Powers*, p. 5.

12. Polly Toynbee, "Sex and death lie at the poisoned heart of religion", *The Guardian online*, 14 September 2010.

13. *ibid.*

14. Polly Toynbee, "We must be free to criticise without being called racist", *The Guardian online*, 18 August 2004.

15. Mark Oppenheimer, "Leaving Islam for Atheism and finding a much needed place among peers", *The New York Times online*, 23 May 2014.

16. Polly Toynbee, "David Cameron won't win votes by calling Britain a Christian country", *The Guardian online*, 14 April 2014.

17. Polly Toynbee, "British universities shouldn't condone this kind of gender segregation", *The Guardian online*, 26 November 2013.

18. Data can be accessed at http://cdn.yougov.com/cumulus_uploads/document/4n6d3tnayp/YG-Archive-University-of-Lancaster-Faith-Matters-Debate-results-180613-faith-schools.pdf (accessed 23 October 2014).

19. Jonathan Hill, *The History of Christian Thought*, Oxford: Lion Hudson 2003, pp. 118–71.

20. Dee Dyas (ed.), *The English Parish Church through the Centuries*, York: University of York 2010, DVD Rom.

21. "Heritage of Mercy" at www.buildinghistory.org (posted 24 June 2006, accessed 21 November 2014).

22. G. E. Evans (ed.), *A History of Pastoral Care*, London, New York: A & C Black 2000.

Chapter 5

1. https://www.churchofengland.org/about-us/facts-stats.aspx (accessed 17 October 2014).

2. Hannah Lambie, *The Trussell Trust Foodbank Network: Exploring the Growth of Foodbanks across the UK*, Coventry: Coventry University 2011, pp. 12–13.

3. Statistics extracted from the Church Urban Fund's report *The Church in Action: A National Survey of Church-led Social Action*, January 2013.

4. For more information on theonomists, or other groups like them, see Richard G. Kyle, *Apocalyptic Fever: End Time Prophecies in Modern America*, Eugene (OR): Wipf and Stock 2012, pp. 212–15.

5. The transcript can be found at http://www.amindatplay.eu/2009/12/02/intelligence²-catholic-church-debate-transcript (accessed 22 October 2014).

Chapter 6

1. Alister McGrath, *Why God Won't Go Away*, London: SPCK 2011, p. vii.

2. Richard Dawkins, "Religion's Misguided Missiles", *The Guardian*, 15 September 2001.

3. Polly Toynbee, "Sex and death lie at the poisoned heart of religion", *The Guardian online*, 14 September 2010.

4. Christopher Hitchens, *God is Not Great*, New York: Atlantic Books 2007, Chapter 2, "Religion Kills".

5. Sam Harris, *The End of Faith: Religion, Terror and the Future of Reason*, New York: Norton & Company 2004.

6. "Afterword" in Sam Harris, *The End of Faith: Religion, Terror and the Future of Reason*, New York: Norton & Company 2005.

7. Julian Glover, "Religion does more harm than good – poll", *The Guardian*, 23 December 2006.

8. Karen Armstrong, *Fields of Blood: Religion and the History of Violence*, New York: Knopf Publishing Group 2014.

9. There are numerous examples, but a recent one would be the biographical story of Nabeel Qureishi in his *Seeking Allah, Finding Jesus*, Grand Rapids: Zondervan 2014.

10. See for example the articles on www.nonresistance.org (accessed 3 November 2014).

11. There are a number of excellent histories of the Crusades, among them one by David Nicolle (Osprey 2001) and another by Jonathan Howard (Golgotha Press 2011), both entitled *The Crusades*.

12. Edward Stourton, *John Paul II: Man of History*, London: Hodder and Stoughton 2006.

13. Michael Howard's *War in European History*, Oxford, New York: OUP 1975 (reprinted 2009) is an excellent thematic approach to covering and analysing the wars that have raged across the continent from the medieval period to the modern day.

14. As the website acknowledges, accurate figures are almost impossible to come by, as there is considerable political milage to be made in exaggeration on all sides. However, as a sense of the difference in scale between "religiously motivated violence" and "power struggles or ethnic violence" it displays the difference very clearly.

Chapter 7

1. Larry Shiner, "The Concept of Secularisation in Empirical Research", *Journal for the Scientific Study of Religion*, Vol. 6, pp. 207–20.

2. Peter Gay (ed.), *The Freud Reader*, New York: W.W. Norton & Co. 1995, p. 435.

3. Sigmund Freud, *An Autobiographical Study*, New York: W. W. Norton & Co. 1989 [1952], pp. 130–31.

4. Such as "Science as a vocation" published after his death (1920) in 1946.

5. William Swatos and Kevin Christiano, "Secularization Theory: The Course of a Concept", *Sociology of Religion*, Vol. 60, Issue 3, Fall 1999, p. 212.

6. Steve Bruce, "Secularisation and Church Growth in the United Kingdom", *Journal of Religion in Europe*, Vol. 6, 2013, pp. 273–96.

7. Jürgen Habermas, *Philosophical – Political Profiles*, Baskerville: MIT Press 1983, p. 82.

8. Charles Taylor, *The Secular Age*, Cambridge (MA): Harvard University Press 2007, p. 15.

9. Charles Taylor, *Secular Age*, p. 727.

10. Daniel Chirot, *Religion and Progress*: From the Enlightenment to the Twenty-First Century, Guiding Paper Series Publication for the Association of Religion Data Archives, no date.

11. Rodney Stark, "Secularization R.I.P.", first published in *Sociology of Religion* (1999) Vol. 60, pp. 249–73; later revised and republished as Chapter 3 of Rodney Stark and Robert Finke, *Acts of Faith*, Berkeley: University of California Press 2000.

12. See for example John Sommerville, "Stark's Age of Faith Argument and the Secularization of Things: A Commentary", *Sociology of Religion*, Vol. 63 Issue 3, Fall 2002, pp. 361–72.

13. *ibid.*, p. 363.

14. John Lawson, *Mediaeval Education and the Reformation*, Abingdon: Routledge 1967 (reprinted 2007).

15. Nick Spencer's excellent book *Atheists: The Origin of the Species*, London: Bloomsbury 2014, generally deals with more modern atheist thought, but it is nevertheless vital reading for those wishing to get a sense of the long view on this phenomenon.

16. Sommerville, "Stark's Age of Faith", p. 363.

17. Charles Hummel, "The Faith Behind the Famous", *Christianity Today* 4 January 1991.

18. Eugene Lyman, "Social Progress and Religious Faith", *Harvard Theological Review* Vol. VII, No. 2, April 2014, pp. 139–65.

19. *ibid.*, p. 140.

20. Michael Mullett, *Martin Luther*, London: Routledge 2004, pp. 164–67.

Chapter 8

1. Christine Barker, "Church State Relationships in German 'Public Benefit' Law", *The International Journal of Not-for-Profit Law*, Vol. 3, Issue 2, December 2000.

2. See Matthias Schulz, "The Last Supper: Germany's Great Church Sell-off" in the *Spiegel online* at http://www.spiegel.de/international/zeitgeist/german-catholic-and-protestant-churches-sell-off-church-buildings-a-883054.html (17 February 2013, accessed 10 March 2015).

3. Sarah Borgloh, *Have You Paid Your Dues?: On the Impact of the German Church Tax on Private Charitable Contributions*, Centre for European Economic Research, January 2009.

4. National Intelligence Council, *Global Trends 2030: Alternative Worlds*, December 2012, p. 14.

5. See Sylvester Ponnumuthan (ed.), *Christian Contribution to Nation Building: A Third Millennium Enquiry*, Cochin 2004.

6. Bielefeldt has said this a number of times – see for example his Statement of the Special Rapporteur on freedom of religion or belief, during the 22nd session of the Human Rights Council. The text is at http://www.ohchr.org/EN/NewsEvents/Pages/DisplayNews.aspx?NewsID=14400&LangID=E (accessed 13 March 2015).

7. OHCHR (Office of the UN High Commissioner for Human Rights), *Rapporteur's Digest on Freedom of Religion or Belief*, 2012, p. 59.

8. There was an article about the launch of "Near Neighbours" by Riazat Butt, "Church of England gets £5m for community cohesion project" in *The Guardian*, 20 February 2011.

9. See http://www.bbc.co.uk/religion/religions/christianity/cofe/cofe_1.shtml (accessed 10 October 2014).

10. This is a paraphrase of the brief history found at https://www.churchofengland.org/about-us/history/detailed-history.aspx (accessed 10 October 2014).

11. The work of the Lords Spiritual is detailed at http://churchinparliament.org (accessed 10 October 2014).

12. Adrian Hamilton, "Will the last person to leave the Church of England please turn out the lights", *The Independent*, 18 April 2011.

13. Douglas Carswell, "The Time is Now Right to Split the Church", *Evening Standard*, 13 June 2012.

14. http://www.secularism.org.uk/disestablishment.html (accessed 10 October 2014).

15. Alexis de Tocqueville, *Democracy in America*, London: Wordsworth 1998.

Chapter 9

1. See www.bbc.co.uk/news/uk-27105023 (dated 21 April 2014, accessed 4 March 2015).

The Atheist Who Didn't Exist

Andy Bannister

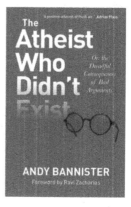

In the last decade, atheism has leapt from obscurity to the front pages: producing bestselling books, making movies, and plastering adverts on the side of buses. There's an energy and a confidence to contemporary atheism: many people now assume that a godless scepticism is the default position, indeed the only position for anybody wishing to appear educated, contemporary, and urbane. Atheism is hip, religion is boring.

Yet when one pokes at popular atheism, many of the arguments used to prop it up quickly unravel. *The Atheist Who Didn't Exist* is designed to expose some of the loose threads on the cardigan of atheism, tug a little, and see what happens. Blending humour with serious thought, Andy Bannister helps the reader question everything, assume nothing and, above all, recognise lazy scepticism and bad arguments. Be an atheist by all means: but do be a thought-through one.

"Intelligent, funny, and elegant."
Michael Coren, author, broadcaster and journalist

"Exactly what this sceptical believer needed."
Drew Marshall, radio host

"Powerful and accessible... profoundly positive."
Dr Peter Riddell, SOAS

"A positive whoosh of fresh air."
Adrian Plass

ISBN 978 0 85721 610 6 | e-ISBN 978 0 85721 611 3

Against the Flow

John C. Lennox

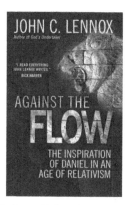

Daniel's story is one of extraordinary faith in God lived out at the pinnacle of executive power. It tells of four teenage friends, born in the tiny state of Judah about twenty-six centuries ago, but captured by Nebuchadnezzar, emperor of Babylon. Daniel describes how they eventually rose to the top echelons of administration.

Daniel and his friends did not simply maintain their private devotion to God; they maintained a high-profile witness in a pluralistic society antagonistic to their faith. That is why their story has such a powerful message for us. Society tolerates the practice of Christianity in private and in church services, but it increasingly deprecates public witness.

If Daniel and his compatriots were with us today they would be in the vanguard of the public debate. What was it that gave that ancient foursome, Daniel and his three friends, the strength and conviction to be prepared, often at great risk, to swim against the flow?

"I highly recommend this book."
Professor J. P. Moreland, Distinguished Professor of Philosophy, Biola University, La Mirada California

"Remarkable."
Jonathan Lamb, CEO, Keswick Ministries

"I cannot think of a more important book for a secular, pluralist age."
Amy Orr-Ewing, Oxford Centre for Christian Apologetics

ISBN 978 0 85721 621 2 | e-ISBN 978 0 85721 622 9

When I Pray, What Does God Do?

David Wilkinson

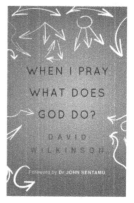

What happens when we pray? Does God always answer? Why does it sometimes feel like he doesn't?

Scientific developments and daily encounters with the pain of unanswered prayer can leave us wondering what to make of the whole topic.

Scientist and theologian David Wilkinson explores these thorny issues, sharing his insights and struggles as he engages with scientific questions, biblical examples, and his own, sometimes painful, experiences of answered and unanswered prayer.

"Profoundly helpful and encouraging to anyone trying to pray with both heart and mind."
Rt Revd John Pritchard, former Bishop of Oxford

"Deeply illuminating and highly accessible."
Most Revd and Rt Hon Dr John Sentamu, Archbishop of York

"This has encouraged, challenged and informed my thinking and practice... I wholeheartedly commend it."
Revd Emmanuel Mbakwe, The Apostolic Church UK

"Combines humour, personal experience, and informed intelligence... an excellent read!"
Joel Edwards, Micah Challenge

ISBN 978 0 85721 604 5 | e-ISBN 978 0 85721 605 2